The Australian Blouse

By Martha Campbell Pullen, Ph. D.

May God Bless You
Martha Pullen

To Kathy

May God Bless You
Martha Pullen
5-5-99

Book Team

Book Design and Layout
Kelly Chambers and Ann Le Roy

Contributing Sewing Designers
Claudia Newton, Sue Pennington, Charlotte Potter, Patty Smith,
Lynn Holyoake, Sheryl Capps, Patti Jo Larson, Marlis Bennett,
Mary Griffin, Kelly Latreille, Linnette Whicker, Chris Tryon

Construction Consultants
Kathy McMakin, Claudia Newton and Charlotte Potter

Illustrated By
Kathy Brower, Kris Broom and Angela Pullen

Photography
Jack Cooper Photography, Jennifer & Company, Christian Lund

© 1998 Martha Pullen Company

Printed By
Lithographics, Inc.
Nashville, TN

Published and Distributed By
Martha Pullen Company, Inc.
518 Madison Street
Huntsville, Alabama 35801-4286
Phone 256-533-9586
Fax 256-533-9630

Library of Congress Catalog Card Number 98-66729

ISBN 1-878048-15-5

Dedication

This book is dedicated to Lynne Wilson Holyoake and her family, David Holyoake, Fiona Elizabeth Holyoake and Belinda Jane Holyoake.

I met Lynne Holyoake the first time I traveled to Australia to teach heirloom sewing at Anne's Glory Box. Since she was a very advanced heirloom stitcher as well as a master embroiderer, I felt I had very little I could teach her; however, she was a wonderful student. We became fast friends and corresponded regularly about sewing and designing. On a later trip, I met her beautiful daughters, Fiona and Belinda at a photo shoot at the Sydney Opera House. I met her wonderful husband, David, on another trip.

Lynne has designed for our magazines and our books on many occasions. I fell in love with the blouse featured in this book after I saw the one Lynne was wearing the first time I met her years ago. After careful examination of the blouse, I remarked to Lynne, "That is the most perfect 'sewing embellishment' blouse that I have ever seen in my life." It has an "embellishment panel" in the front as well as the back. It is very flattering for all figure types because of its style, and it can be worn on the outside or tucked in.

I told her, "Lynne, you must consider letting us do something to get that blouse out all over the world." The first time we used the blouse, graciously given by Lynne, was in the 300 Martha's Sewing Room television series. The book sold very quickly and was soon out of print. It seemed like everybody in the country, after seeing the fashion show that featured these blouses, wanted the book.

About the time we ran out of the book, the machine embroidery craze hit the world and I realized that the blouse was also perfect for machine embroidery as well as hand embroidery. We then asked our sewing machine companies to embellish a blouse to be included in the new book. Of course, we also wanted to include the original blouse found in the television series. The blouse in this book was one of Lynne's many designs which she has used for teaching classes to women all over Australia and the world. Lynne now teaches this blouse, and many other things, at our Martha Pullen Schools of Art Fashion here in Huntsville. Actually Lynne attended our school here in Huntsville several times and it became apparent to me that she should be teaching, not studying with us.

Lynne is the middle child and only daughter of Enid and Charles Wilson, who have both died in recent years. Lynne misses them so much and greatly appreciates their love and complete support and encouragement while she was growing up. Lynne attended the Presbyterian Ladies College in Sydney form the age of 6 to 17 years where she received the finest education possible.

She learned sewing at a very early age. Lynne began her teaching career in the in her early teens. She taught Sunday school until she left for nursing training. She completed 4 years of nursing training at St. Luke's Anglican Hospital in Sydney. She believes that nursing equips one for everything life has to hand out. Living in the hospital nursing home taught her how to deal kindly with other people. Lynne and one of her dear friends used to sew clothes until all hours of the night. This friend is still nursing and told Lynne recently, "I envy your life of sewing and teaching sewing."

After Lynne completed her nursing training, she became a hostess for Quantas airways. In those days, the hostess was like the purser; she looked after documentation, mothers and babies, and helped with the first class meals. She stayed with Quantas for 3 1/2 years until she met her soul mate, David Holyoake. In those days, one could not be a hostess

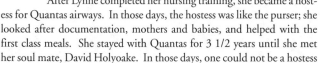

if one married. She resigned to marry David, and is very glad that she did not travel during those early years of marriage. She says, " How lucky one is to be able to cement one's marriage in those early years. I have been allowed to grow and achieve because of the help and support David gives me and I am so thankful for this."

Fiona Holyoake arrived five years after Lynne and David were married and two years later, Belinda Jane Holyoake arrived. Like all mothers who love to sew, the first thing you think of when you have a baby girl is pink, lace, smocking beautiful fabric and pretty things for this darling baby. She bought a blue - cased Elna SU and enrolled in classes. Like so many mothers, she'd sew late into the night so she could take them to church in new outfits. The wonderful thing about sewing for your small children is the fact that if the outfit isn't quite perfect, they don't mind wearing it and you gain confidence from mistakes and practice.

Lynne attended technical college in Australia for about seven years to complete a garment assembly and pattern making certificate course. Like most women, she has been through many phases of sewing including quilting, but she feels fortunate to have found heirloom sewing. Lynne feels that it allows one to be so creative and allows one to add a very special touch to blouses, nighties, children's clothing and christening dresses. Lynne also loves embroidery by hand and machine. Another passion is shadowwork embroidery because it complements any garment so beautifully. She always tells her students that embroidery is the icing on the cake.

When she finished her study of sewing at the technical college, she was fortunate enough to be asked to do a lot of teaching. Lynne believes that one can learn and grow through teaching; she is convinced that we learn so very much from our students, and that teachers get back one- thousand- fold more than they give. She tries to be generous, inspirational, and giving in her classes; that is her philosophy of education. She is busy with teaching or with projects at least five days a week and her mind works "faster than my abilities." She teaches in the city and country areas of New South Wales. Her students are often isolated and they absolutely adore the sewing sisterhood.

Lynne makes mention of a mentor in sewing, Robin Holden, who is also a very special friend. She helped Lynne sew in her early years of teaching at the Crewel Gobelin. Robin gave Lynne the inspiration for this blouse in this book and Robin kept the students coming to Lynne's classes.

Fiona is now 24 years of age and is a chartered accountant. Belinda is 22 and has just finished with honors in Marketing. Both are beautiful, young women and Lynne and David are so proud of them. While recently in Sydney, I had the privilege of having dinner with the whole family and I absolutely adore the girls and David. We talked so much during the meal that we closed the restaurant. Lynne, Fiona and David have visited in our home in Huntsville and Belinda has an open invitation, of course.

Lynne wrote to me, "I love David who has always supported me and I know how blessed I am. My girls have always loved my clothing and have been supportive of my career also. I thank God for giving me a talent and allowing me to share it with others."

Table of Contents

Introduction To Blouses

One of the most popular designs we ever published was the Lynne Holyoake blouse, or the Australian Blouse, featured in this book. The *Martha's Sewing Room* television show guide (300), which contained the original blouse, sold out almost as soon as women paged through the book. We even had to stop taking the blouses with us when we traveled because people wanted to buy "that Australian blouse" pattern and we had no books to sell. When machine embroidery came into popularity, everybody who saw the original blouse said, "Oh, Martha, that is the perfect machine embroidery blouse." I agreed completely and began itching to do gorgeous, EASY machine embroidery down the front panel. (You know how much I love the word easy.) Women began to use this blouse as their machine embroidery canvas with thread as their paint, and we met one woman who used this pattern to make a memory blouse to wear for her parents' anniversary. She transferred black and white pictures of them during their early years to make a photographic keepsake of their lives together on the panels and sleeves. Shaped lace insertion accented the black and white photo transfers, which were gorgeous against the white silk dupioni background.

We were determined not to disappoint those who did not yet have the pattern, and in order to provide more creative ideas for those who already had the pattern, this book was compiled. It includes all of the great original versions as well as new machine-embroidered versions. This blouse really is the perfect showcase for all types of creative designing, and a wonderful place to use the amazing embroidery capabilities of those magnificent new sewing machines. For those of you who love to scan and create original designs with computers, this blouse is perfect for that also. Creativity is one of the main reasons that I sew, and with the mere push of a button, the new machines provide unlimited possibilities for creativity. What fun! Our sewing machine companies have enthusiastically contributed to the making of this book by using our pattern, fabric of their choice, and built-in embroidery designs to create elegant blouses. I would like to thank Baby Lock, Bernina, Elna, New Home, Pfaff, Singer and Viking for their participation.

Not only is the Australian Blouse perfect for embellishment, it looks great in all sizes; it can be made longer and worn on the outside, or made like the original to be tucked in. Speaking of sizes, we took the original pattern and added one more size for the new book to bring you women's sizes 6-28. In addition to the seven new blouses designed by the machine companies, the book also includes complete instructions and templates for the original variations. The embellishment techniques include French waterfall, shadow shapes, Seminole patchwork, linen transformation, puffing, spoke collar, cutwork, ribbon and organdy sandwich, Normandy lace, and a pink linen version with a hand-embroidered heart/bow motif.

For women all over the world, this is a must-have blouse pattern. We are happy to bring it to you in a larger size range and with many more variations for your enjoyment. ✖

General Machine Embroidery Directions

I. Preparing the Fabric for Embroidery

1. Cut a rectangle of fabric 3" larger than the blouse front pattern piece on all sides.
2. Starch and press the fabric.
3. Trace the outline of the blouse front pattern onto the fabric using a fabric marker or fabric pencil. Also mark the stitching lines and center front of the blouse pattern piece (fig. 1).

II. Creating Embroidery Templates

If clear plastic templates are not available for the embroidery designs being used, templates can easily be made by stitching the design onto organdy.

1. Using a fine-tip permanent marker, draw vertical and horizontal center lines onto a piece of organdy that is larger than the hoop (fig. 2).
2. Place the organdy in the hoop, matching the vertical and horizontal lines with the vertical and horizontal centers of the hoop. The organdy should be taut and without wrinkles.
3. With the permanent marker, trace all the way around the inside of the hoop. Write "top" and "right side" at the very top of the hooped organdy (fig. 3). Also note if any changes are made before beginning to stitch, such as rotating the design 90° or moving the hoop up/down or side to side before beginning to stitch.
4. Stitch the embroidery with a contrasting color; it may be necessary to use tear-away stabilizer under the hooped organdy, or a wash-away stabilizer on top and/or bottom of the organdy. When the embroidery is complete, unhoop and cut along the outline of the hoop (fig. 4).
5. Place the organdy template to the blouse fabric with the embroidery design in the desired location. Add stabilizer, if needed. (Refer to III. Stabilizing, for stabilizing options). Using a few pins, pin the organdy template to the blouse fabric (fig. 5). Hoop the fabric, using the outer edges of the organdy template as a placement guide (fig 6). Follow any directions written on the organdy template, then remove the organdy template. Stitch the embroidery onto the fabric (fig 7).

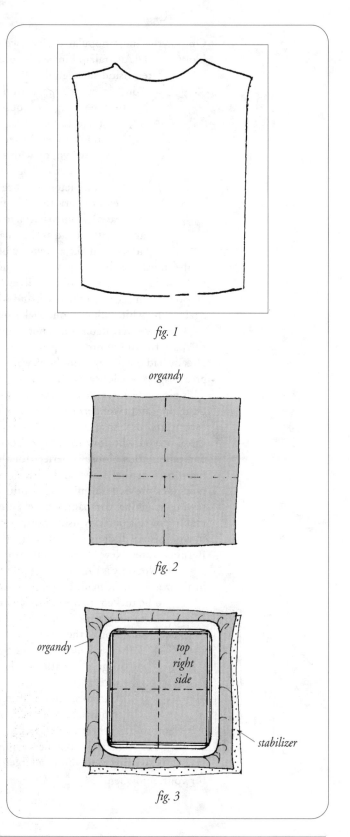

fig. 1

organdy

fig. 2

organdy

top right side

stabilizer

fig. 3

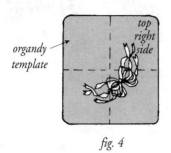

fig. 4

Place the design in the desired location.

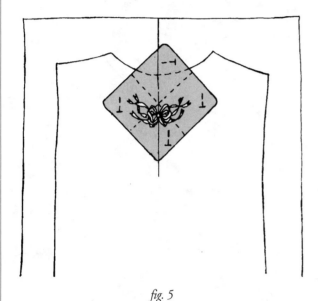

fig. 5

Hoop using the organdy template as a guide.

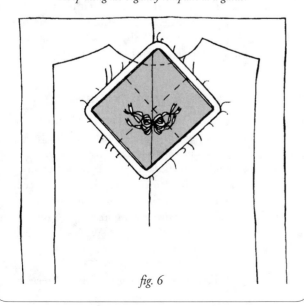

fig. 6

III. Stabilizing

Sometimes the fabric is stabilized and then hooped. Other times the fabric is hooped and a stabilizer is placed under the hooped fabric. Whatever the case may be, stabilizer is almost always used to create a smooth, flat base for the embroidery.

a. Starch - Most fabrics can be starched for the first "layer" of stabilization. Check the fabric for spotting before the starch is used to stiffen the fabric.

b. Spray-on stabilizer - Spray-on stabilizer, such as Sullivan's Fabric Stabilizer, is heavier than starch and is excellent for lighter embroidery. Check the fabric for spotting before the spray-on stabilizer is used to stiffen the fabric.

c. Water-soluble stabilizer (WSS) - WSS can be placed on top of the fabric, on the bottom of the fabric or the fabric can be sandwich between layers of WSS. (Note: A temporary spray adhesive, such as KK2000 or ATP 505 can be used to hold the WSS to the fabric.) Hoop the fabric with the WSS in the desired location. When the fabric to be embroidered is netting, sandwich the netting between two layers of WSS. Adding WSS to the top and bottom of the netting adds the perfect amount of stabilization. WSS is washed away after the embroidery is completed.

d. Tear-away stabilizer - This stabilizer is placed under the hooped fabric. When the stitching is complete, the stabilizer is carefully torn from behind the embroidery.

e. Cut-away stabilizer - The fabric-type stabilizers work very well to stabilize an opaque fabric. This stabilizer is a poly-mesh material that can be temporarily secured to the wrong side of the fabric with a temporary spray adhesive. The fabric is then embroidered and the excess stabilizer is cut away from behind.

Remove the organdy template to stitch.

fig. 7

Baby Lock Embroidered Motif Blouse

by Kelly Latreille
of the Baby Lock

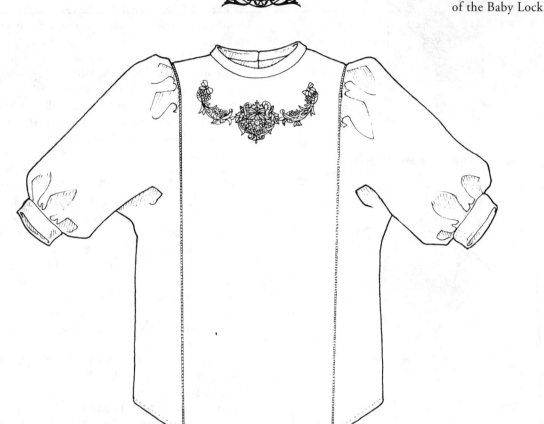

Swiss embroidered motifs have been loved for over one hundred years in the heirloom sewing industry. If you can find them, they are very expensive! The good news is that if you have a Baby Lock (Esanté) machine you can embroidery your own! Our Baby Lock designer has embroidered three gorgeous Swiss motifs onto organdy, cut them out, and appliquéd them onto the front of this fabulous pink silk dupioni blouse. She has also cut a straight one-inch ring collar to attach to the neckline, demonstrating another lovely way to use this Australian Blouse pattern. Another delicate feature is the wing-needle machine entredeux stitched onto a strip of fabric just like Swiss entredeux. This perfect strip of Baby Lock entredeux has been inserted into the side seams. The Baby Lock blouse is certainly a lovely interpretation of our blouse pattern!

Supplies

✳ Baby Lock Èsante sewing/embroidery machine
✳ Embroidery Cards: Lace Card #29
✳ Fabric: Pink silk dupioni and white organdy
✳ Thread color and type: Metrosene #60 wt.- white

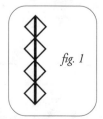

fig. 1

Specific Information

Motifs from lace card #29 were used on this blouse. The motifs were stitched onto organdy, trimmed from the organdy and appliquéd to the blouse. To create a see-through appearance, the silk fabric was trimmed from behind the motifs. Machine-made entredeux was placed in the seams, giving the blouse that special heirloom effect. The entredeux was made with a wing needle and the utility stitch illustrated in fig. 1 (S.L. = 2.5, S.W. = 4.0). A Baby Lock serger was used to gather the sleeves.

Construct the blouse using the General Blouse Directions.

Bernina Flowers and Faux Smocked Trim

by Marlis Bennett of
Bernina of America

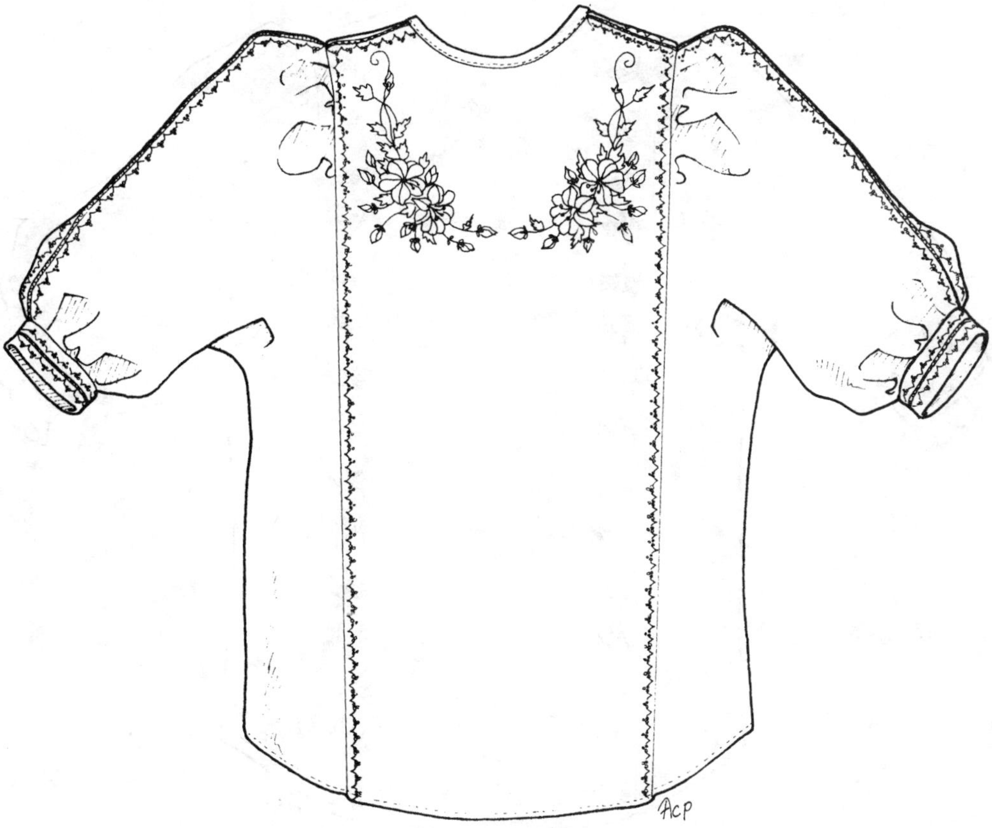

It is not an exaggeration to describe this blouse by Bernina as simply gorgeous. Colors of ecru, pale peach, and several shades of green are blended on the front in a mirror-imaged floral embroidery design which is a beautiful addition to the off-white silk dupioni. The green decorative stitch, used along the panel seams and the center sleeve seams, actually looks like hand smocking. Machine fagotting is used to join the shoulder and side seams; it really looks like hand fagotting, yet it is made on the Bernina! The cuffs are also embellished with the same faux smocking and machine fagotting. Use the interesting heirloom stitches on your Bernina to re-create this on this gorgeous blouse, and get ready to receive rave reviews!

Supplies

- Bernina *artista* 180E sewing/embroidery machine
- Embroidery Module Design Packet 1
- Large Hoop
- Hoop Template
- Fabric: White Silk Dupioni
- Thread color and type:
  - Sulky #1082 - soft white
  - Sulky #1017 - pale peach
  - Sulky #1064 - peach
  - Sulky #1209 - soft sage green
  - Sulky #1063 - mint
  - Sulky #1508 - sage
  - Sulky #1180 - soft taupe brown
- Additional sewing machine feet used in construction: Tailor Tack Foot - #7, Bias Binder 26-30mm and Foot #94, Open Embroidery Foot #20

Specific Information

The rose floral design from embroidery module design package 1 was chosen to embellish this blouse front. The design was rotated 180° for the left motif; the design was rotated 180° and mirror-imaged for the right motif. To stabilize the fabric, the wrong side of the upper front panel area was sprayed with spray adhesive and a poly-mesh stabilizer was applied. The blouse was constructed using decorative machine fagotting in the shoulder and sleeve seams; this technique was also used in the cuff embellishment. Decorative stitch #601 was used to delicately frames the front panel. Binding the neck was a snap with the bias binder foot.

Construct the blouse using the General Blouse Directions.

Elna Embroidered Blouse with Pleated Cuffs

by Chris Tryon
of Elna USA

What could be more elegant than ecru silk dupioni embroidered with darker beige machine embroidery? The Elna blouse is decorated with an elegant, stylized leaf design which borders the front panel on each side. This is a very flattering and slenderizing treatment, emphasizing the up and down lines of the body. There is a sophisticated companion design embroidered near the neckline. The sleeve cuff is purchased ecru ribbon which matches the color of the darker beige embroidery on the front of the blouse; little dupioni pleats are stitched to the bottom of the purchased ribbon for a true designer treatment. This sophisticated heirloom blouse, made on your Elna, will be a joy to wear.

Supplies

✳ Elna CE20 sewing/embroidery machine
✳ Embroidery Card: Australian Flowers
✳ Fabric: Ecru silk dupioni
✳ Thread color and type: Sulky 40 wt. in shades of ecru to complement fabric color

Specific Information

The Australian Flower embroidery card was used create the beautiful embellishment on the blouse. Designs #23, #24, and #25 were combined to produce the center design. Designs #17 and #18 were alternated down each side of the front panel. Pleated fabric ruffles, made with the ruffler, were used to embellish the cuffs, which were made of purchased ribbon.

Construct the blouse using the General Blouse Directions.

New Home Fabulous Flowers

by Sheryl Capps of New Home
Sewing Machine Company

The lavish embroidery over the entire front panel of this ecru linen blouse is just breathtaking. Beige-toned flowers, leaves, stems and several tiny flowers flow gracefully from the top of the panel to the bottom. On the cuffs, more beautiful flowers are embroidered. Some of the flowers look like little pinwheels and fans; some are traditional shapes and look like beige poinsettias. A diverse variety of leaves completes the tone-on-tone embroidery. Embroidering with one tone is very elegant, really showing off the stitching and the variety of flowers and leaves. The intricate details of the embroidery draw you in for a closer look, and the binding around the neckline is completely hidden for a flawless finish. What a gorgeous blouse, showing off embroidery in a fabulous way on this New Home beauty.

Supplies

* New Home-Janome *Memory Craft* 9000 sewing/ embroidery machine
* Embroidery Card: # 119 - Australian Floral Designs
* Template (included with the embroidery card)
* Fabric: Ecru Linen
* Thread color and type: Janome embroidery thread, color #223 (beige gray)

Specific Information

All the designs on card #119 were used on the blouse except the bow (pattern 6). The templates included with the memory card were used for design placement. The cuff was embroidered with pattern #1 in the center and pattern #4 on either side of the center design.

Construct the blouse using the General Blouse Directions.

Pfaff Embroidered Delicate Designs

by Linnette Whicker of the
Pfaff American Sales Corp.

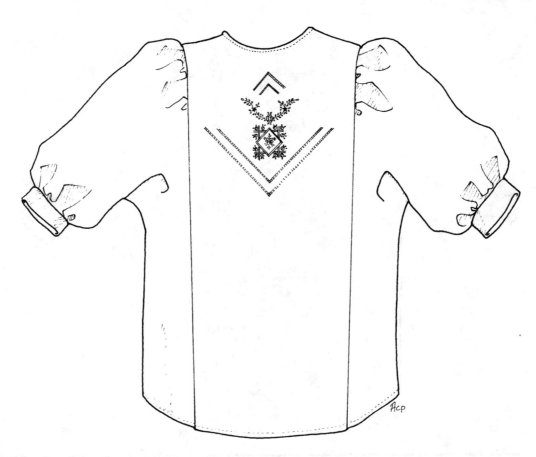

Using pink, ecru and robin's egg blue thread on pale ecru linen, our Pfaff designers have embroidered an exquisite selection of designs on the front of a very versatile Australian Blouse. Pink V shapes are repeated at both the top and the bottom of the design, with small shapes at the top and larger shapes at the bottom; both are worked in a beautiful entredeux stitch. A graceful spray of ecru and pink flowers with robin's egg leaves arches above a beautiful square design featuring the same flowers and leaves. I especially love the flowers in these designs; they look like hand embroidery. What a wonderful way to enjoy heirloom embroidery with the Pfaff machine! Made of linen as shown, the blouse is perfect to wear with jeans, a khaki skirt, a wool skirt or slacks, or silk pants. Paired with a simple matching skirt, this blouse in any type of fabric would make the perfect bridesmaid's ensemble.

Supplies

❋ Pfaff 7570 sewing/embroidery machine
❋ Embroidery Card: Scattered Flowers #28
❋ Hoop 120
❋ Fabric: Ecru Linen
❋ Thread color and type:
    Alcazar 30 wt. #556 - beige   #444 - pink   #736 - green

Specific Information

Patterns #17 and #18 from embroidery card #28 were used to decorate the blouse front. After the two embroidery designs were completed, a ruler and a fabric marker were used to draw small "V's" above the designs and larger "V's" were drawn below the designs. The lines were then stitched with a #100 wing needle using stitch #111 (W = 2.0, L = 2.5, tension +3) with foot 2A centered on the lines. The construction of the blouse was completed on the serger. NOTE: To pivot at the point of the "v", use the tie-off key to complete a stitch, then pivot the fabric with the needle in the down position. The needle will now be in the "front" hole of the last stitch. Reposition the needle to the "back" hole of the stitch and continue sewing forward with the foot centered on the drawn lines.

Construct the blouse using the General Blouse Directions.

Singer Floral and Hemstitched Fantasy

by Mary Griffin of the
Singer Sewing Company

Two very unusual ideas are combined in this fantasy blouse from Singer, made of blue-green linen embroidered in gorgeous teal thread. Don't you just love the wide scallops on the shoulders? The shoulder stitching also features a wing-needle baby daisy and featherstitching. The motif at center front is accented with a circular scallop. Little flowers trail off to the side, a large flower is embroidered at the top, and a beautiful flower and leaf scroll completes the bottom. The flower and leaf scroll was also used on the cuff. It is absolutely fascinating to look at the stitches on the stems; some are triple stitched and some are satin stitched. This Singer blouse is truly a fantasy of wing-needle decorative stitches, as well as bold satin stitch.

Supplies

✽ Quantum XL-1000 sewing/embroidery machine
✽ Embroidery Cards: "Country Kitchen" (No. 1)
   "Gigantic Florals (No. 15) "Country & Garden" (No. 14)
✽ Fabric: Blue-green linen
✽ Thread color and type: Sulky #1046
✽ Additional sewing machine attachments used for
   embellishment: Circular Stitch Ruler

Specific Information

Martha's books were the inspiration for the Singer Floral and Hemstitched Fantasy blouse. Designs were selected from three embroidery cards: "Country Kitchen" (No. 1),

"Gigantic Florals (No. 15) and Country & Garden" (No. 14). The selected designs were programmed into the "Multiple Embroidery" mode, mirrored-imaged, rotated and positioned in the desired location. Multi-hooping ensured that the patterns aligned perfectly. The machine was converted to regular sewing to complete the final touches. The Circular Stitch Ruler was used to stitch the circle of decorative stitches around the center flower. The shoulder embellishment was created with a lacy scallop stitched diagonally. The star stitch with a #19 wing needle and a decorative stitch (regular needle) were alternated to decorate the fabric above the scallops.

Construct the blouse using the General Blouse Directions.

Viking Embroidered Netting Lace

by Patti Jo Larson
of Husqvarna Viking

The Viking designer chose white English cotton netting for this stunning masterpiece which gives the appearance of being circa 1900. A motif embroidered in white runs down both sides of the front panel. This same motif, mirrored, creates ovals down the center front. White cotton French lace insertion covers the seams on the front of the blouse as well as the back. Because this blouse is a truly French-sewn creation, the neckline and the sleeve cuffs are finished with entredeux and gathered French lace. An off-white camisole is used under this sheer blouse, adding to the antique effect. What a perfect blouse to be worn with a water-stained taffeta skirt for a wedding or with black wool pants for any dressy event. Using the gorgeous embroidery stitches on your Viking, you can make this Victorian, turn-of-the-century embroidered heirloom in your sewing room today.

Supplies

✳ Viking #1+ sewing/embroidery machine
✳ Embroidery Card: #24 (designs by Martha Pullen)
✳ Fabric: White Netting
✳ Thread color and type: Mettler 60 weight, color #703

Specific Information

The designs on this blouse are from card #24 (Martha Pullen). The plus hoop allows for two motifs to be stitched before re-hooping. Design 24:31 is used throughout the blouse front with colors #2 and #3 only. The center design is made narrower to overlap better. The settings for the center design are as follows: Design 24:31, S.L. = 4.0, S.W. = 3.5. The large netting rectangle for the blouse front was stabilized by sandwiching the netting between two layers of water-soluble stabilizer.

Construct the blouse using the General Blouse Directions.

General Blouse Directions

Fabric Requirements

All sizes: 2³/₄ yards

Spoke Collar: Size 2-12 = ¹/₂ yards, Size 14-28 = ³/₄ yards

Stand-Up Collar: Interfacing ¹/₄ yard

Lace and Trims Requirement - Refer to specific directions under each blouse title.

The ladies blouses are sized as follows:

XXS = 2-4	M = 14-16
XS = 6-8	L = 18-20
S = 10-12	XL = 22-24
XXL = 26-28	

All pattern pieces are found on the pattern pull-out.

All seams ¹/₄". Overcast the seam allowances using a zigzag or serger. French seams can be used, if desired. When tracing a design or pattern piece use a water or air soluble pen or pencil.

Very Important: Read both the general directions and the specific directions before cutting or sewing the blouse desired. The general directions list the order for stitching and the specific directions provide the embellishment techniques with any change in the general directions required to complete the blouse.

I. General Cutting and Sewing Directions

1. Fold the selvages to the center of the fabric. Cut out the bodice front and bodice back from each fold. Transfer all markings (**fig. 1**).

2. Cut out four side/sleeve pieces. Transfer markings to these pieces.

3. If cuffs are used to finish the ends of the sleeves, cut two cuffs 4¹/₂" wide to the following measurements:
Size XXS (2-4) = 11¹/₂", Size XS (6-8) = 12", Size XXL = 14¹/₂"
Size S (10-12) = 12¹/₂", Size M (14-16) = 13",
Size L (18-20) = 13¹/₂", Size XL (22-24) = 14"

4. If the stand-up collar is used to finish the neck, cut two collars.

5. Cut one fabric piece 3" by 10" for the back placket.

Note: Any additional pieces needed for a specific blouse will be listed under each blouse title.

6. Embellish the blouse front using the specific directions under each dress title.

7. Back Placket: Finish two long sides and one short of the rectangle using the following technique: turn the edges of the two long sides to the inside ¹/₈" and ¹/₈" again and stitch in place. Repeat for one short side. Note: these sides can be finished with the serger (**fig. 2**).

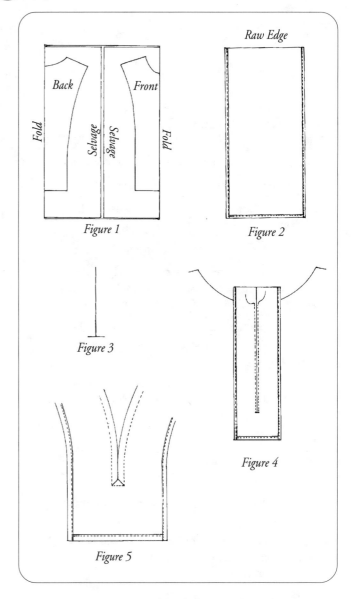

Figure 1

Figure 2 — Raw Edge

Figure 3

Figure 4

Figure 5

a. On the wrong side of the placket piece draw a line down the center stopping 2" from the lower edge. Place a ¹/₄" line (¹/₈" on each side of the center line) at the bottom of the center line creating a small upside-down "T" (**fig. 3**).

b. Place the right side of the placket piece to the right side of the blouse back, centering the drawn line of the rectangle to the center back of the blouse. The rectangle should extend beyond the top edge of the blouse at least 1". Pin in place.

c. Starting at the neck, stitch ¹/₈" from the center line. Stitch to the lower line, pivot, stitch across the lower line, pivot, and stitch ¹/₈" from the line to the top of the blouse (**fig. 4**).

d. Cut down the center line stopping ¹/₄" from the lower stitching. clip from the center line to each corner (**fig. 5**).

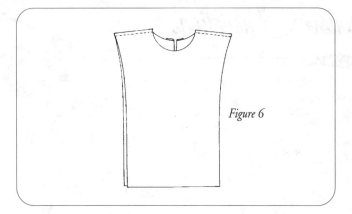

Figure 6

e. Flip the placket to the inside of the blouse and press.

f. Trim the top of the placket to fit the neck of the blouse.

8. Place the blouse front to the blouse back at the shoulders and stitch using a $^1/_4$" seam (**fig. 6**).

9. Neck - Refer to the specific neck finishes in II.

10. Sleeves - Place two sleeve pieces, right sides together, at the top center and stitch together using a $^1/_4$" seam (**fig. 7**). The underarm seam will be stitched later. Repeat for the other sleeve.

   a. Run two gathering rows $^1/_8$" and $^1/_4$" between the marks on each sleeve. Repeat the gathering along the lower edge of the sleeve (**fig. 8**).

   b. Match the marks of the front and back and seams to the side/sleeve pieces. Stitch in place using a $^1/_4$" seam (**fig. 9**).

11. Finishing the Sleeves - Refer to the specific directions for sleeve finishes.

12. Place the sides of the blouse together and stitch using a $^1/_4$" seam (**fig. 10**).

13. Hem the bottom of the blouse turning the edge to the inside $^1/_4$" and $^1/_4$" again. Press and stitch in place (**fig. 11**).

14. Add a hook and eye to the back neck to close the blouse. If a stand-up collar is used place two hooks and eyes at the top and bottom of the collar.

II. Neck Finishes

A. Bias Facing

Supplies: No extra supplies required.

1. Measure the length around the neck of the blouse. Cut a bias strip $1^1/_4$" wide by the length around the neck plus 1".

2. Fold the bias facing strip in half and press.

3. Place the raw edges of the strip to the right side of the blouse at the neck edge. The facing strip should extend beyond the back openings $^1/_2$" on each side (**fig. 12**).

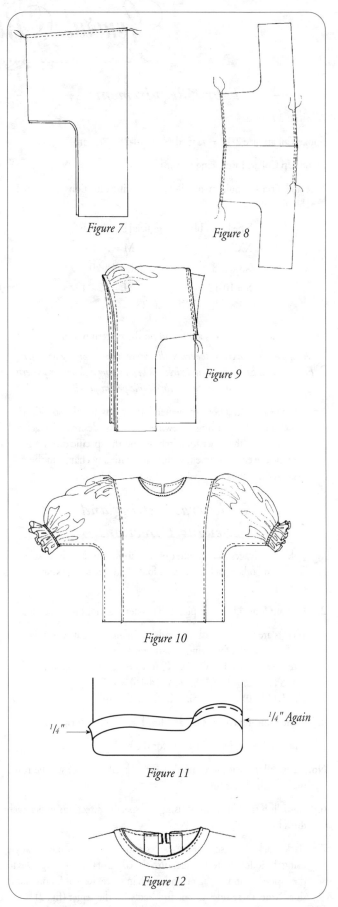

Figure 7

Figure 8

Figure 9

Figure 10

$^1/_4$" ◄———   ———► $^1/_4$" Again

Figure 11

Figure 12

4. Stitch along the neck edge using a $1/4$" seam. Trim the seam to $1/8$" and clip the curves.

5. Pull the facing away from the blouse. Turn the extended edges to the inside. Fold the facing completely to the inside of the blouse and stitch in place by hand or machine (**fig. 13**).

B. Bias Binding

Supplies: No extra supplies required.

1. Measure the length around the neck of the blouse. Cut a bias strip 2" wide by the length around the neck plus 1".

2. Fold the bias facing strip in half and press.

3. Place the raw edges of the strip to the right side of the blouse at the neck edge. The strip should extend beyond the back openings $1/2$" on each side (**refer to fig. 12**).

4. Stitch along the neck edge using a $1/2$" seam. Trim the seam to $1/4$".

5. Pull the binding away from the blouse. Turn the extended edges to the inside. Fold the binding over the $1/4$" seam allowance. Hem the binding to the inside of the neck by hand or machine (**fig. 14**).

C. Entredeux and Edging Lace

Supplies: $3/4$ yard entredeux and $1^1/2$ yards edging lace

1. Measure the length around the neck of the blouse. Cut a strip of entredeux to this length plus 1".

2. Cut one side of the fabric completely away from the entredeux. Cut a piece of edging to twice the length of the entredeux. Gather the edging to fit the entredeux. Stitch the entredeux to the gathered edging using the technique entredeux to gathered lace (**fig. 15**).

3. Cut clips along the remaining fabric side of the entredeux (**fig. 16**). Place the clipped edge to the right side of the neck. $1/2$" tabs will extend past the folded back edges of the bodice.

4. With a $1/4$" seam, stitch the entredeux/gathered lace in place using the technique entredeux to fabric (**fig. 17**).

5. Flip the entredeux/gathered lace away from the blouse. Fold the entredeux/lace tabs to the inside of the blouse.

6. Stitch this seam allowance to the dress using a small zigzag. This makes the lace stand up at the neck and tacks the entredeux/lace tabs in place (**fig. 18**).

D. Stand-Up Collar

1. Cut two collars (one collar and one lining). Interface the collar piece. Place the collar to the blouse neck right sides together with $1/4$" of the collar extending past the center back opening. Stitch to the blouse using a $1/4$" seam. Clip the seam allowance (**fig. 19**).

2. Fold the lower edge of the collar lining to the inside $1/4$" and press. Place the collar lining to the collar, right side together. Stitch around the outer edge of the collar using a $1/4$" seam. Trim the seam to $1/8$". Clip the curves (**fig. 20**).

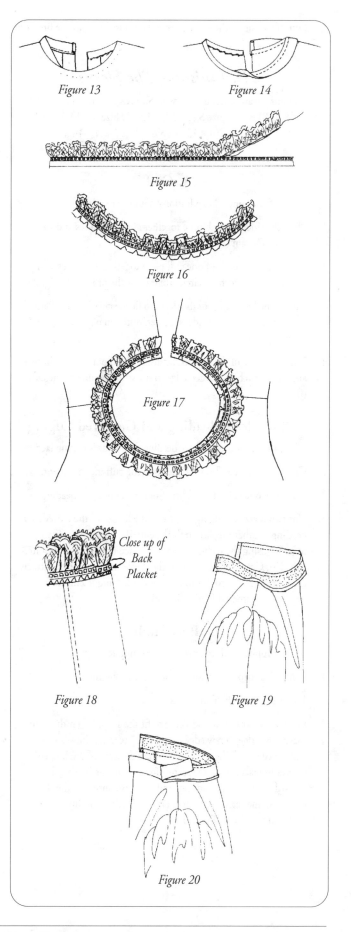

Figure 13

Figure 14

Figure 15

Figure 16

Figure 17

Close up of Back Placket

Figure 18

Figure 19

Figure 20

3. Flip the lining to the inside. Hem the pressed fold of the lining to the collar stitching line (**fig. 21**).

III. Finishing The Sleeve

Cuff Measurements (cut two): Size XXS (2-4) = $11^1/_2$",
Size XS (6-8) = 12", Size S (10-12) = $12^1/_2$", Size M (14-16) = 13",
Size L (18-20) = $13^1/_2$", Size XL (22-24) = 14",
Size XXL (26-28) = $14^1/_2$

A. Cuff

Supplies: No additional supplies required.

1. Place the sides of the blouse together along the sides and stitch using a $^1/_4$" seam (**refer to fig. 10**).

2. Place the short ends of one cuff piece together and stitch using a $^1/_4$" seam. This forms a circle. Repeat for the other cuff (**fig. 22**).

3. Gather the lower edge of the sleeve to fit the circular cuff. Place the cuff to the sleeve, right sides together. Stitch in place using a $^1/_4$" seam (**fig. 23**).

4. Turn the edge of the cuff to the inside $^1/_4$". Fold the cuff in half and hand stitch the folded edge to the stitching line of the cuff (**fig. 24**).

B. Entredeux/Beading and Gathered Edging

Supplies: 1 yard entredeux/beading and 2 yards edging lace

1. Cut two entredeux/beading pieces to the cuff measurement.

2. Cut away one side of the fabric from the entredeux/beading.

3. Cut two pieces of edging lace twice the length of the entredeux/beading. Gather the lace to fit the entredeux/beading. Zigzag together using the technique gathered lace to entredeux/beading (**fig. 25**). Gather the bottom of the sleeve to fit this strip. Attach the strip to the sleeve bottom using the technique entredeux/beading to gathered fabric (**fig. 26**).

C. Bias Binding

Supplies: Fabric only (no extra supplies required).

1. Cut a bias strip $2^1/_4$" wide by the cuff measurement.

2. Fold the strip in half and press.

3. Gather the bottom of the sleeve to fit the strip. Stitch the strip in place, raw edge to raw edge, using a $^1/_2$" seam. Trim seam allowance to $^1/_8$" (**fig. 27**). Stitch the side seam of the bodice/sleeves in place. With the seam allowance of the binding pressed toward the binding, fold the binding to the inside of the sleeve enclosing the seam allowance. Hand stitch the binding to the inside of the sleeve (**fig. 28**). ※

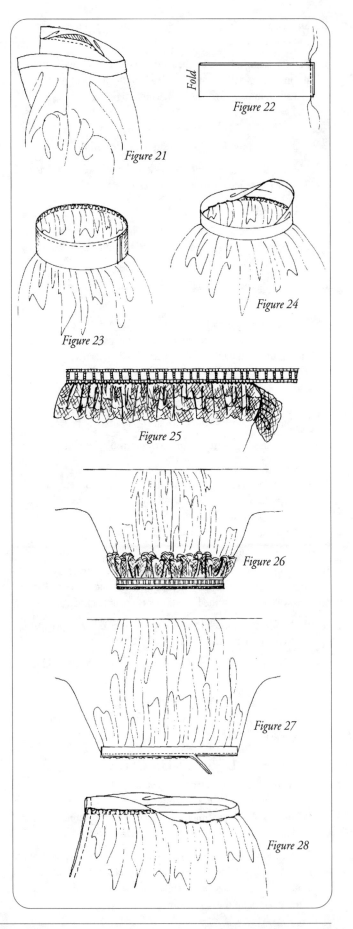

Figure 22

Fold

Figure 21

Figure 23

Figure 24

Figure 25

Figure 26

Figure 27

Figure 28

French Waterfall Blouse

Beautifully done in medium blue and white Swiss Nelona batiste, this blouse is a Victorian delight. The center panel of this wonderful blouse is of blue Nelona: the white lace is scalloped down the front of this blouse on both sides, giving the effect of a French waterfall. Three rows of scalloped double needle pintucks follow the outlines of the scallops. Entredeux is in the seams of this blouse and makes a pretty finish to join the blue and white batiste. On the puffed sleeves, scallops join the white sleeve to the blue batiste; three rows of pintucks follow the scalloped lace on the blue batiste. A blue cuff finishes the sleeve. The neckline is finished with entredeux/gathered lace trim. The back of the blouse is totally white batiste; once again entredeux is found between the seams.

Directions

Follow the General Blouse Directions found on page 15. Embellishment directions are given below.

Materials Needed

✳ 2¹/₂ yards white Nelona

✳ ³/₄ yard blue Nelona

✳ Waterfall template for sleeves and front on pattern pull-out.

✳ Double needle for pintucks

✳ Stabilizer- if wing needle work is used for decoration

✳ 3¹/₄ yards entredeux

✳ 1¹/₄ yards 1" edging lace

✳ 4 yards ³/₄" insertion lace

✳ Scallop template can be found on the pull-out.

Embellishing the Blouse Front

1. Trace the blouse front on a rectangle of blue Nelona at least 5" wider than pattern piece.

2. Trace off neck and shoulders at the top of the rectangle.

3. Trace scallop design (French waterfall) on blue blouse front, starting at the shoulder, 2" from the neck edge.

4. Shape lace along the scallops using the technique for scalloped lace found on page 48 in the technique section of this book.

5. Stitch both sides of scallops to the blue blouse front with a zigzag or a wing needle/entredeux stitch. Remember to use stabilizer if wing needle/entredeux is the stitch of choice. If desired, trim the fabric from behind the lace.

6. Stitch three pintucks along the outer edge of the scalloped lace using the techniques for curved pintucks found on page 38. The tucks on the front of this blouse start ³/₈" from the lace and are ¹/₄" apart. Press the pintucks away from the lace.

7. Place the front blouse pattern on the embellished rectangle matching the neck and shoulders. Cut out.

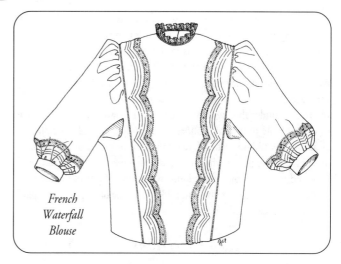

French Waterfall Blouse

8. Stitch the front to the back at the shoulder seams.

9. Stitch entredeux along the sides of the blouse front/back using the technique "entredeux to flat fabric." Transfer the sleeve markings to the entredeux.

10. Refer to the general directions for the sleeves. Gather the sleeves to fit the entredeux with the marks of the sleeves to the marks of the bodices. Attach the sleeves/sides to the blouse using the technique "entredeux to gathered fabric."

Neck Finish

Refer to the II. Neck Finishes - C. Entredeux and Edging Lace found on page 17.

Embellishing and Finishing the Sleeves

1. Cut a strip of blue Nelona fabric 4" wide by the width of the bottom of the sleeve.

2. Trace the scallop template design along the top of the strip with the upper edge of the curve along the top of the strip.

3. Shape lace along the template lines using the technique for scalloped lace found on page 48.

4. Stitch the scallops in place only along the lower edge of the lace.

5. Place three pintucks below the lace scallops. Refer to the pintucking directions above Embellishing the Blouse Front - step 6.

6. Trim the fabric from behind the lace.

7. Place the blue fabric/lace strip along the bottom of the white sleeve. Place the edge of fabric strip to the edge of the sleeve.

8. Stitch along the upper edge of the lace scallops. Trim the excess white fabric from behind the lace.

9. To finish the sleeves refer to the General Directions III. A. Cuff. found on page 18. ✺

Shadow Shapes Blouse

Combining organdy, lace insertion, lace edging, and silk ribbon embroidery is what makes this blouse fit for a royal occasion. Ecru is the color; Swiss Nelona batiste is the fabric. The curved upper section of the bodice is Nelona with an organdy overlay. Shaped in a wonderful loop in the middle and going over to the shoulders is an ecru lace insertion about ⅝ inch wide. This same dark ecru lace insertion is under the organdy which is the top layer of the cuff. Once again this same treatment is under the organdy on top of the collar. Beautiful silk ribbon embroidery is found in the center of the collar and cuffs, in the points where the lace shapes meet at the top of the loop and in the top of the lace loop on the center front of the blouse. The colors in the silk ribbon embroidery are pale blue, pale pink, pale yellow, leaf green, and white.

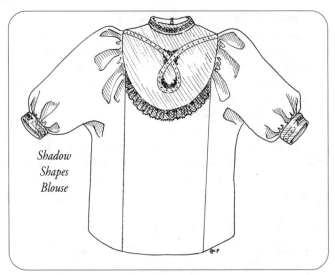

Shadow Shapes Blouse

Directions

Follow the General Blouse Directions found on page 15. Embellishment directions are given below.

Materials Needed

✳ 2¾ yards Nelona

✳ ½ yard organdy

✳ 1 yard of 1" edging lace

✳ 2¾ yards of ⅝" insertions lace

✳ Silk Ribbon: Pink # 122, Green # 062, White # 3, Light Yellow # 12, Yellow # 121 and Blue # 10.

✳ Lace loop template and embroidery design found on pull-out.

Embellishing the Blouse Front

1. Cut the bodice front from the batiste. Place the lace loop template 2" from the center front neck line. Trace the lace loop template and the edging lace curve on the blouse front.

2. Shape the lace insertion along the loop template lines following the directions for lace shaping.

3. Stitch both sides of the lace in place using a small zigzag. Place a rectangle of organdy over the shaped lace on the blouse front. The organdy must extend beyond the edging lace curve template and the upper edges of the bodice. Pin in place along the neck, shoulders and sides.

4. Using a small zigzag, stitch the organdy to the blouse front along edging lace curved template. Trim the excess organdy below the curve.

5. Gather the edging lace and place just above the zigzag on the template. Zigzag the lace in place. Treat as one layer of fabric.

6. Construct the blouse bodice and side/sleeves as referred to in the general directions.

Neck Finish

1. Cut two stand-up collars from batiste (inner collar and collar lining) and one stand-up collar from organdy.

2. Center a piece of insertion lace on the right side of the batiste inner collar. Stitch both edges of the lace to the collar piece.

3. Place the organdy collar over the lace/inner collar. Pin in place and treat as one layer of fabric.

4. Construct the collar using the general blouse directions II. Neck Finishes - D. Stand-Up Collar found on page 17.

Finishing the Sleeves

1. Cut out two cuffs from batiste and two cuffs from organdy.

2. Repeat the following directions for the two cuffs. Fold the cuff in half and press to crease the center. Mark the seam allowance along the upper edge of the cuff. Center the insertion lace between the fold and the seam allowance mark. Stitch in place along each side of the lace.

3. Place the organdy on top of the batiste cuff and treat as one layer of fabric.

4. Stitch the cuffs to the sleeves using the general blouse directions III. Finishing the Sleeves - A. Cuffs found on page 18.

Silk Ribbon Embellishment

Trace and stitch the embroidery design on the blouse front, sleeves and collar. ✳

Seminole Patchwork Blouse

Using one of my favorite fabrics, ecru silk dupioni, this blouse is fashioned very simply with two strips of seminole patchwork traveling from the front to the back. The patchwork is in shades of dark ecru, forest green, burgundy, and dark teal. The cuffs are one and three quarters inches wide; the collar is one inch wide. The back closing is a placket and it closes with a hook and eye. Probably you can see by now that this blouse offers an almost endless range of possibilities for not only heirloom sewing, but also any type of embellishment which you enjoy making. The center panel is the perfect place for embroidery, patchwork, lace shaping, painting, appliquéing, or other needlearts. That is the reason we chose this blouse pattern to go along with the book in this series!

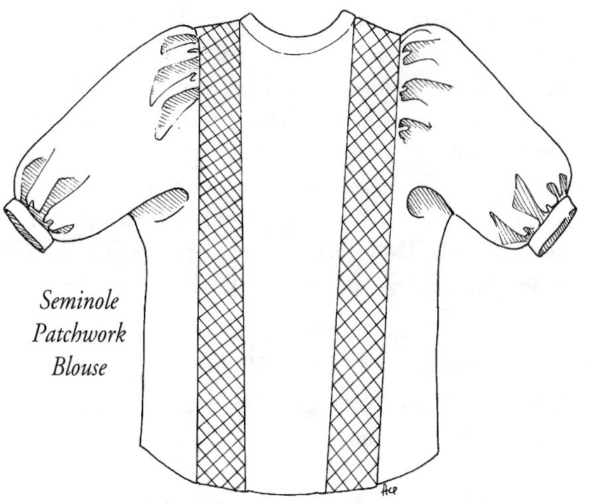

Seminole Patchwork Blouse

Directions

Follow the General Blouse Directions found on page 15. Embellishment directions are given below.

Materials Needed

- 3 yards ecru silk
- 1/4 yard burgundy
- 1/4 yard green
- 1/4 yard teal
- 1/2 yard bronze

Embellishing the Blouse Front

1. Refer to the Seminole patchwork directions found on page 61. Making the Seminole patchwork strips for the blouse - Cut six 1 1/4" by 45" pieces of the following colors: burgundy, teal, and green. Cut twelve pieces 1 1/4" wide by 45" of bronze fabric. Cut twelve pieces 1 1/2" by 45" of ecru. Seven pieces of fabric will be stitched together to form six multi-colored strips. Note: cutting needs to be very precise.
2. Stitch the pieces together in the following sequence to form one multi-colored strip 45" long (all seams 1/4"): ecru, bronze, green, burgundy, teal, bronze, ecru. Repeat for the other strips. Note: Stitching needs to be very precise.
3. Cut across each multi-colored strip to create 1 1/4" pieces.
4. Place two multi-colored pieces, right sides together, lining up the seams, off setting each piece by one square. In other words match the following colors of each piece:

Piece #1		Piece #2
ecru	to	bronze
bronze	to	green
green	to	burgundy
burgundy	to	teal
teal	to	bronze
bronze	to	ecru

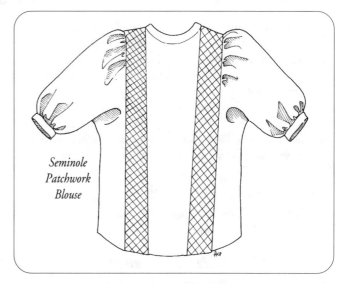

Pin in place. Stitch together using a 1/4" seam.

5. Repeat for the remaining pieces. When the strip is turned vertically each color lines up, top to bottom. The unstitched pieces on each side of the patchwork piece will be trimmed off when the piece is complete.
6. Trim off each side of the patchwork strip 1/4" from the points of the bronze square.
7. Cut out the bodice front and back. Stitch the bodices together at the shoulders using a 1/4" seam.
8. Trim 3" from each side of the front/back bodice. Stitch the patchwork strip to the sides of the front/back bodice.
9. Attach the sleeves referring to the general directions Step 10.

Neck Finishes

Refer to the general blouse directions II. Neck Finishes - D. Stand-Up Collar.

Finishing the Sleeves

Refer to the general blouse directions III. Finishing the Sleeves - A. Cuffs.

Wedding Blouse

What a delightful combination is white silk dupioni and English cotton embroidered netting lace. The sleeves are finished with entredeux beading and gathered wide English netting lace. If this blouse were used for a wedding attendant's outfit, the brides favorite color ribbon could be run through the beading in the sleeves. Or several colors of ribbons taken from the colors in the bouquet of flowers which the bridesmaids carried could be run through and tied in a multi-color bow. The gathered English netting is found once again around the neckline, and the collar finishes off this area.

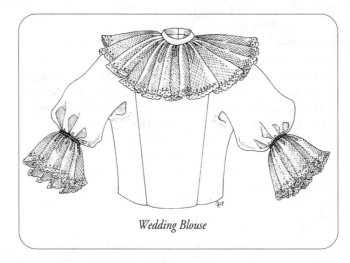

Wedding Blouse

Directions

Follow the General Blouse Directions found on page 15. Embellishment directions are given below.

Materials Needed

❋ 2³/₄ yards White Silk Dupioni

❋ 4 yards of 7" 7" wide English embroidered netting

❋ 1 yard Entredeux Beading

Embellishing the Blouse Front

This blouse has no embellishment except the gathered English embroidered netting collar and sleeve ruffles. Refer to the general blouse directions on page 15 to construct the blouse front, back and sleeves.

Neck Finish

1. Cut a piece of lace 2 yards long. Finish the two short sides of the ruffle by turning the edge to the inside ¹/₈" and ¹/₈" again and stitching in place.

2. Fold lace in half and mark the center. Run two gathering rows ¹/₈" and ¹/₄" from the top edge of the lace.

3. Gather the lace to fit the neck of the blouse. Match the center of the blouse with the center mark of the lace and match the finished edges of the lace with the edges of the back opening. Baste the collar in place along the ¹/₄" gathering line.

4. Attach stand-up collar to the blouse neck using the general directions II Neck Finishes - D. Stand-Up Collar found on page 17.

Finishing the Sleeves

Before stitching the underarm seam of the blouse finish the bottom of the sleeve using the following directions:

1. Cut two pieces of lace 1 yard* each. Run two gathering rows ¹/₈" and ¹/₄" from the top edge of the lace.

2. Cut two strips of entredeux beading to the following measurements: Size 2 & 4 = 11¹/₂", Size 6 & 8 = 12", Size 10 & 12 = 12¹/₂", Size 14 & 16 = 13", Size 18 & 20 = 13¹/₂", Size 22 & 24 = 14".

3. Gather the lace to fit the entredeux beading. Attach the gathered lace to the entredeux beading using the technique entredeux to gathered fabric found on page 32.

4. Attach the lace and beading strip to each sleeve using the technique entredeux to gathered fabric.

5. Stitch the underarm seam in place to finish the sleeve. ✠

Linen Transformation Blouse

Simple and very easy to make is this version of our series blouse. A doily is simply stitched to the center front of the blouse; linens cover the collar and cuffs also. Ecru Nelona Swiss batiste is the fabric for the blouse. Several different types of old linens are also used in the blouse. The doily is embroidery plus tatting. The neckline lace is Battenburg and the lace on the sleeves is cluny. Please do mix and match your laces on any garment that you make. I used to have a little theory that I shared with my students. When one makes French garments for the first time, she always matches the pattern of lace. When one has stitched French dresses for years, she mixes anything but the kitchen sink in one dress. Either way is beautiful, of course, but being creative is usually more fun. Your taste in the lace selection is really the only thing that matters.

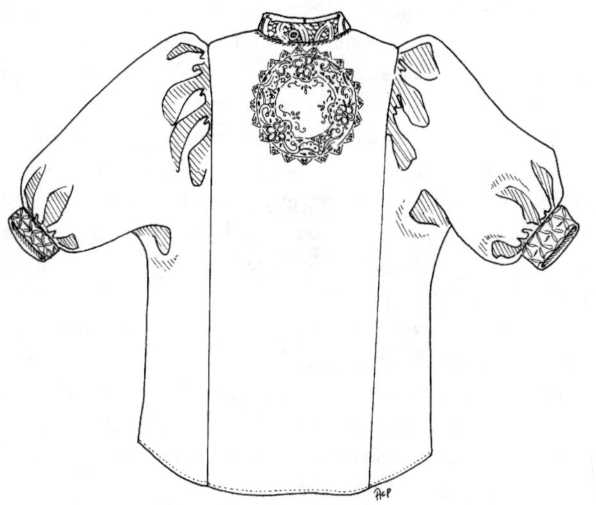

Linen Transformation Blouse

Directions

Follow the General Blouse Directions found on page 15. Embellishment directions are given below.

Materials Needed

- $2^3/_4$ yards Nelona Swiss batiste
- Round 8" circumference crocheted doily
- $1^1/_2$ yards lace trim to cover cuffs and collar

Note: Crocheted placemats, Battenburg placemats or doilies may also be used to cover cuffs and collar.

Embellishing the blouse front

1. Cut out the blouse front.
2. Stitch the round doily $1^1/_4$" from the center front of the blouse neck edge.

Neck Finish

1. Cut collar according to the general blouse directions.
2. Cover one collar piece with lace trim and pin in place. Treat as one layer.
3. Complete the collar using general directions II. Neck Finishes - D. Stand-Up Collar found on page 17.

Embellishing the Cuff

1. Cut cuffs according to the general pattern directions.
2. Cover cuffs with lace trim of your choice.
3. Pin in place and treat as one layer of fabric
4. Complete cuffs using the general blouse directions III. Finishing the Sleeve - A. Cuffs found on page 18.

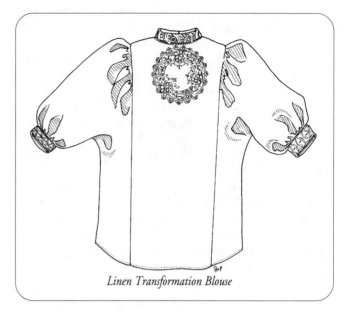

Lynne Holyoake Puffing Blouse

Since Lynne designed the blouse for this series, she consented to make several of the blouses. This linen beauty is loaded with gorgeous details including a strip of puffing down the center front. Swiss faggotting is found on either side of this puffin. Next comes a strip of Swiss embroidered insertion which has white-on-white lilies of the valley for its main design. Triple entredeux runs vertically on the outside of this embroidered insertion and a lone vertical pintuck is next. Machine wing needle entredeux is stitched beside the vertical side seams . The sleeves are gorgeous with faggotting stitched in the exact center of the sleeve. On either side of the faggotting are one pintuck, one row of machine wing needle entredeux, three pintucks, another machine wing needle entredeux, three more pintucks and one last row of machine wing needle entredeux. The cuff on the sleeve has three rows of pintucks next to the gathered portion of the sleeve and one row of machine wing needle entredeux below that. Handkerchief linen makes the most wonderful heirloom blouses; this one is elegant and easy to wear to many different occasions.

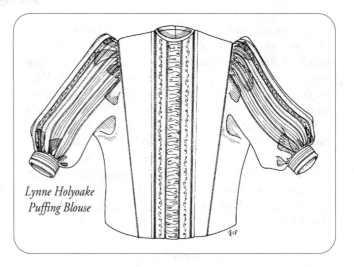

Lynne Holyoake
Puffing Blouse

Directions

Follow the General Blouse Directions found on page 15. Embellishment directions are given below.

Materials Needed

❋ 2³/₄ yards white handkerchief linen
❋ 1¹/₂ yards of 2¹/₂" wide white on white embroidered insertion
❋ 1¹/₂ yards triple entredeux
❋ 1¹/₂ yards faggoting
❋ 1 yard Swiss white on white insertion (1" wide, excluding seam allowances) with faggoting or entredeux on both sides
❋ Wing needle (100 size)
❋ Double needle (2.0)

Embellishing the Blouse Front

1. Cut the following into 27" pieces:

   a. Two pieces triple entredeux

   b. Two pieces 2¹/₂" wide embroidered insertion

   c. Two pieces faggoting

2. Cut one fabric strip 3" wide by 45" long for puffing.

3. Using a gathering foot, gather each side ¹/₂" from the cut edges. Finished puffing will measure about 27" long. For further puffing instructions, please turn to the puffing section in the technique portion of this book. Optional: If a gathering foot is not used, two rows of gathering stitches can be run in each side of the strip and then pulled up to 27". Please note: If Swiss batiste is used rather than the linen, more than 45" may be required for the puffing

strip. The lighter weight fabric (Swiss batiste) gathers up more when using the gathering foot than a medium weight fabric (linen).

NOTE: The strips of laces, fabric and puffing will be stitched together to create a rectangle larger than the pattern piece. After the rectangle is created, the bodice front will be cut from the created fabric rectangle.

4. Creating the rectangle - Attach faggoting to each side of the puffing strip using the technique entredeux to gathered fabric.

5. Attach embroidered insertion to each side of the faggoting strip using the technique entredeux to flat fabric.

6. Attach triple entredeux to each side of the embroidered insertion pieces using the technique entredeux to flat fabric.

7. Cut two strips of fabric 6 inches wide by 27" long and attach a fabric strip to each side of the triple entredeux using entredeux to flat fabric.

8. Place one double needle pintuck ³/₈" from the triple entredeux. This completes the rectangle. Starch and press.

9. Cut out the blouse front from the created rectangle.

Neck Finish

1. Refer to the general blouse directions II. Neck Finishes - B. Bias Binding found on page 17.

Embellishing and Finishing the Sleeves

1. Cut two strips of the one inch wide Swiss insertion 18" long.

2. Stitch two sleeve pieces on either side of an 18" strip of Swiss insertion. This put the insertion down the center of the sleeve. Repeat for the other sleeve. ❈

3. Repeat the following stitch pattern on each side of the insertion for each sleeve. Stitch one double needle pintuck 3/8" away from the insertion. Stitch wing needle entredeux 3/8" from the double needle pintuck. Skip 1" and stitch another row of wing needle entredeux and repeat a third row 1" away from the second. This will create three rows of wing needle entredeux.
4. Place three double needle pintucks 1/4" apart in the center of the two spaces created by the wing needle entredeux.
5. Attach sleeve to bodice referring to general blouse directions step 10 and 11 on page 16.
6. Stitch wing needle entredeux along the bodice front and back at the side/sleeve seams.
7. Place the sides of the blouse right sides together and stitch using a 1/4" seam.

Finishing the Sleeves

Refer to the general blouse directions III. Finishing the Sleeves - A. Cuff found on page 18.

Repeat the following embellishment for each cuff. After cutting the two cuffs, stitch three double needle pintucks 1/4" apart starting 1/2" from one cut edge. Stitch one row of wing needle entredeux 3/8" below the last tuck. This decorates the top side of the cuff. Stitch each cuff in a circle and place to the sleeve as stated in the cuff directions.

Cutwork Blouse

Another of my favorite blouse fabrics, white handkerchief linen, is used for this statement of simplicity. A beautiful dark goldish/tan cutwork design is found on the center front panel. The cutwork design has three teardrops with Richelieu bars below the teardrops. That is the only embellishment on this tailored blouse. The sleeves have a 1 3/4" cuff and the neck has a simple bias binding. Once again showing the versatility of this blouse pattern, it is the perfect garment for those who don't wear lace. It is as dressed up or dressed down as the occasion requires.

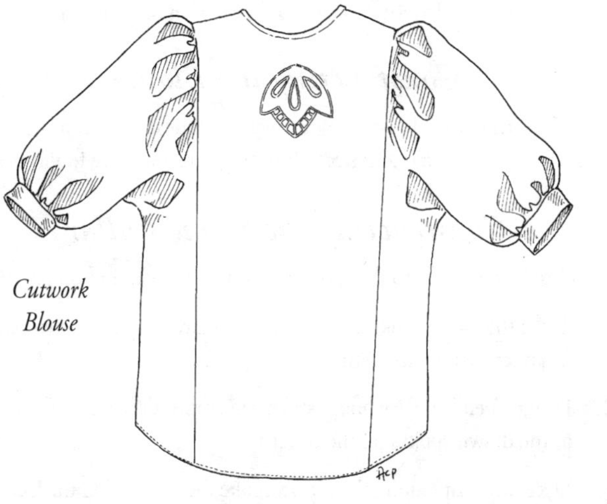

Cutwork Blouse

Directions

Follow the General Blouse Directions found on page 15. Embellishment directions are given below.

Materials Needed

- 2 1/2 yards linen
- Gold cotton embroidery thread
- Cutwork design found on pull-out
- Water Soluble Stabilizer
- Cutwork template can be found on the pull-out.

Embellishing the Blouse Front

1. Trace the blouse front on a rectangle of linen, 1" longer and wider than the pattern piece.
2. Trace the cutwork design in the center of the blouse front beginning 1 1/2" from the neck edge of the blouse.
3. Stitch the cutwork design following the general cutwork directions found on page 53.

Neck Finish

Refer to the general blouse directions II. Neck Finishes - B. Bias Binding found on page 17.

Finishing the Sleeves

Refer to the general blouse directions III. Finishing the Sleeve - A. Cuff found on page 18.

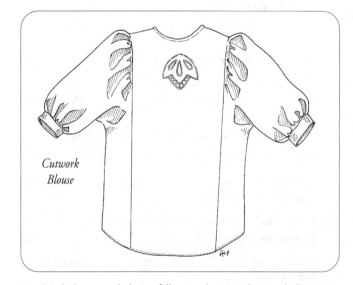

Spoke Collar Blouse

Scalloped spoke collars are among my favorite things for children and adults. This beauty, made of white Nelona, has lovely white-on-white embroidery in each spoke. A wing needle pinstitch is used to attach the lace and to embellish along the sides of each spoke. Gathered lace edging is stitched around the bottom of the scalloped collar. Inside of each spoke is a delicate white on white hand embroidery. The embroidery design consists of four white bullion roses, stem stitches, and lazy daisies. In the words of Margaret Boyles, "There is nothing ever any more elegant than white on white." I think this blouse is certainly a lovely example of white on white simplicity and beauty.

Directions

Follow the General Blouse Directions found on page 15. Embellishment directions are given below.

Materials Needed

❈ 2¹/₂ yards white Nelona

❈ 7 yards of 1" lace edging

❈ 2¹/₂ yards of ⁵/₈" lace insertion

❈ Collar Pattern and embroidery design on pull-out.

Constructing the Blouse

Construct the blouse using the general blouse directions found on page 15. The collar and sleeve finishing directions are found below.

Constructing the Spoke Collar

For illustrations, refer to the spoke collar directions found on page 63.

1. Trace the entire spoke collar pattern on a rectangle of Swiss batiste 2" larger than the pattern.

2. Using an embroidery hoop, stitch the embroidery in each section of the drawn spokes on the collar.

3. Place lace strips along the drawn spoke lines centering the lace strip on the line.

4. Stitch along each side of the lace using wing needle entredeux or a small zigzag.

5. Shape insertion lace along the lower edge of the collar using the technique for lace shaping along a scalloped skirt found on page 48. Pin in place.

6. Stitch along the upper edge of the lace using a zigzag or wing needle entredeux stitch. Purchase entredeux can be used if desired.

7. Cut a piece of edging lace 5 yds. long. Gather the edging to fit the back and lower edges of the collar.

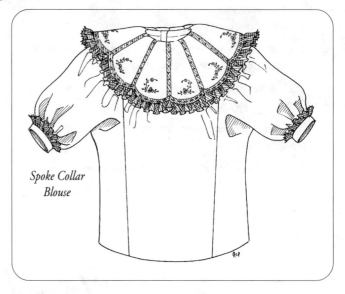

Spoke Collar Blouse

8. Butt the lace edging to the lace insertion and stitch in place using wing needle entredeux or a zigzag. Trim away the excess fabric behind the lace. Cut out neck opening.

9. Place the wrong side of the collar to the right side of the blouse. Pin in place.

10. Attach the collar to the blouse using the general blouse directions II. Neck Finishes - A. Bias Facings found on page 16.

Finishing the Sleeves

1. Refer to the general blouse directions III. Finishing the Sleeves - A. Cuff found on page 18.

2. Cut two pieces of edging lace 1 yd. long. Overlap the ends of the lace and zigzag together.

3. Gather the edging lace to fit the cuff. Place the edging to the seam on the cuff and the sleeve. Zigzag the edging in place on top of the cuff where it meets the sleeve. ❈

Ribbon and Organdy Sandwich Blouse

Blue, green, lavender and yellow ombre ribbons peek through the white Swiss organdy to make an organdy and ribbon sandwich. Gorgeous white Nelona Swiss batiste is the fabric for the blouse with the covering on the center section of the series blouse made of white Swiss organdy. The ombre ribbon has been flip flopped into a beautiful bow with streamers flip flopped down the front of the underneath section. Organdy, once again, makes the top fabric for the ribbon to peek through around the cuffs. Entredeux is used in the front and back vertical seams as well as gathered French lace edging. An entredeux/gathered French edging finish is used on the neckline as well. Sure to be a show stopper, this blouse is also easy to make.

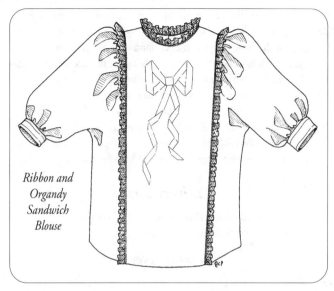

Ribbon and Organdy Sandwich Blouse

Directions

Follow the General Blouse Directions found on page 15. Embellishment directions are given below.

Materials Needed

✳ 2³/₄ yds. white Swiss Batiste (Nelona)

✳ ³/₄ yds. white Swiss organdy

✳ 3 yds. 1" wide ribbon

✳ 3¹/₄ yds. entredeux

✳ 7¹/₂ yds. of 1" edging lace

✳ Ribbon and Organdy Sandwich Bow template found on pull-out.

Embellishing the Blouse Front

1. Cut one blouse front from batiste and one blouse front from organdy.

2. Trace the bow template on the right side of the batiste blouse front with the center of the bow 4" from the center of the neck edge.

3. Shape ribbon along the template lines using the technique for the flip-flop bow found on page 44.

4. Straight stitch along the outer edges of the ribbon and along the inside edges of the bow loops.

5. Place the organdy blouse front over the batiste blouse front. The bow will be between the two pieces. Pin together and treat as one layer of fabric.

Constructing the Bodice

1. Cut out the blouse back. Stitch the front to the back at the shoulder seams.

2. Stitch entredeux along the sides of the blouse front/back using the technique entredeux to flat fabric.

3. Gather the sleeves to fit between the marks of the front/back bodices. Attach the sleeves/sides to the blouse front/back using the technique entredeux to gathered fabric.

4. Cut two pieces of edging lace 3 yds. long. Gather the edging to fit the entredeux. Place the gathered lace to the entredeux along the side/sleeves. Butt to the entredeux and zigzag in place.

Neck Finish

Refer to the general blouse directions II. Neck Finishes - C. Entredeux and Edging Lace found on page 17.

Finishing the Sleeves

1. Cut out two cuffs from batiste and two cuff pieces from organdy.

2. Repeat the following directions for the two cuffs. Fold the cuff in half and press. Mark the seam allowance along the upper edge of the cuff. Center the ribbon between the fold and the seam allowance mark. Stitch in place along each side of the ribbon.

3. Place the organdy on top of the batiste cuff and treat as one layer of fabric.

4. Stitch the cuffs to the sleeves using the genreal blouse directions III. Finishing the Sleeves - A. Cuffs found on page 18. ✄

Normandy Lace Silk Dupioni Blouse

One of my all time favorite fabrics is silk dupioni. Normandy lace is lace which has been shaped on netting. In this case, it has been stitched on the center front bodice of our blouse for this series. We have used both lace insertion and lace edging for the lace shaping. This ecru silk dupioni blouse lends itself beautifully to the different shades of ecru laces craftily shaped on top of the ecru netting. The center shaped piece is a pretty bow with long bow ties curved around the bottom of the shaping. In the side seams there is a simple piece of ecru entredeux. The sleeves have a narrow bias binding for their finish. The back has a placket with a pearl button and loop for fastening.

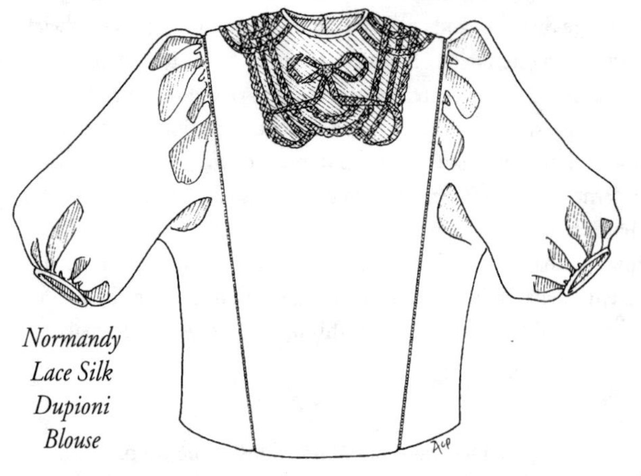

Normandy Lace Silk Dupioni Blouse

Directions

Follow the General Blouse Directions found on page 15. Embellishment directions are given below.

Materials Needed

- ❋ $2^3/_4$ yards ecru silk Dupioni
- ❋ $^1/_3$ yard cotton netting
- ❋ 2 $^2/_3$ yards ecru entredeux
- ❋ 2 yards $^3/_8$" ecru lace insertion
- ❋ $^2/_3$ yard of $^1/_4$" ecru lace insertion
- ❋ $^2/_3$ yard of $^1/_2$" ecru lace edging
- ❋ $^2/_3$ yard of $^5/_8$" ecru lace edging
- ❋ $^2/_3$ yard of $^3/_8$" edging
- ❋ Normandy lace template found on pull-out
- ❋ Water Soluble Stabilizer

Note: This is a great blouse to use your lace scraps. The widths of lace given above are suggestions. You can use other widths of your choice.

Embellishing the Blouse Front

1. Trace the neck and shoulders of the blouse front to a 12" by 15" rectangle of netting.
2. Trace the Normandy lace design on the netting referring to the directions found in the Normandy lace section of this book on page 59.
3. Shape the lace along the template lines using the lace shaping directions in this book.
4. Stitch the laces to the netting referring to the Normandy lace directions on page 59.
5. Do not stitch along the outer edges of the Normandy lace design.
6. Stay stitch around neck and shoulder lines of the netting.
7. Trim netting just above the staystitch lines and from the outer edge of the lace.
8. Cut blouse front from silk Dupioni.
9. Place Normandy lace design on the blouse front, lining up neck edges and shoulders.
10. Pin in place. Straight stitch along the outer edge of the lace.
11. Trim the silk from behind the netting $^1/_4$" from the straight stitch. Clip the remaining $^1/_4$" seam allowance so that it can be pressed toward the blouse. Using a small zigzag, re-stitch along the outer edge of the Normandy lace design. Trim any excess seam allowance that extends below the zigzag.
12. Cut out the blouse back. Stitch the front to the back at the shoulder seams.
13. Stitch entredeux along the sides of the blouse front/back using the technique entredeux to flat fabric.
14. Attach the sleeves/sides of blouse front using the technique entredeux to gathered fabric.

Neck Finish

Bias binding directions found in general blouse directions on page 17.

Finishing the Sleeves

Refer to the general blouse directions III. Finishing the Sleeves - C. Binding found on page 18. ❋

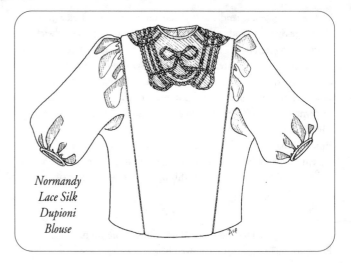

Pink Linen Heart/Bow Embroidered Blouse

A truly unusual masterpiece by Lynne Holyoake is this pink linen blouse. The embroidery design on the front is in shades of pink, white, pale green, medium green, and yellow. The embroidery stitches are French knots, colonial knots, bullion roses, bullion rosebuds, bullion daisies, and stem stitches. The stitches are so very tiny and so delicate! Notice the bow is really two hearts with a heart in the middle for the bow tie. The streamers are stitched in this incredible embroidery. The embroidery is only the beginning of the joy of this masterpiece! There are triple lace hearts on each sleeve. Two are sideways and one is in the middle. All of the lace hearts are outlined with a beautiful machine pin stitch. Pink linen double needle pintucks are in the middle of the heart on the sleeve. Three double needle pintucks are at the bottom of the sleeve and on the cuff there are five more double needle pintucks. There is a row of pink machine pin stitches at the bottom of the cuff.

Running down the two side seams in the front is a row of double needle pintucks and a row of machine pin stitching is right on top of the seam. Traveling over the shoulder and ending a few inches from the shoulder on both the front and back is a piece of lace insertion stitched down with machine pin stitch. At the bottom of the back placket is another beautiful heart stitched down with machine pin stitch and filled with double needle pintucks. What an incredible blouse for a beautiful Christmas celebration or any other type of event. This blouse with a beautiful pink linen skirt would be absolutely elegant for a mother of the bride or groom outfit. I can think of no more fabulous going away outfit for a bride than this blouse with a pretty skirt.

Directions

Follow the General Blouse Directions found on page 15. Embellishment directions are given below.

Materials Needed

✳ 2¹/₂ yards pink linen

✳ Lace template for sleeves found on pull-out

✳ Embroidery template for back heart found on pull-out

✳ Double needle for pintucks

✳ Stabilizer- if wing needle work is used for decoration

✳ 3¹/₂ yards of ⁵/₈" insertion lace (outer sleeve hearts and back heart)

✳ 1 yard of ¹/₂" insertion lace (inner hearts)

Embellishing the Blouse Front and Back

1. Trace the blouse front on a rectangle of linen.

2. Trace heart embroidery design on the center of the blouse rectangle with the center of the heart 4" from the neck edge.

3. Place the design in a hoop and complete the embroidery.

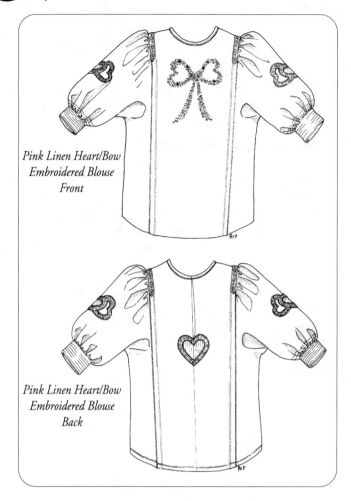

Pink Linen Heart/Bow Embroidered Blouse Front

Pink Linen Heart/Bow Embroidered Blouse Back

4. Cut out the blouse front and back and stitch together at the shoulders. Refer to the general directions for the back placket.

5. Trace the lace heart for the center back just below the back opening. Shape the lace heart using the lace shaping directions found on page 40. Stitch the outer edges of the heart using a zigzag or wing needle hem stitch. Trim the fabric behind the lace. The fabric inside the heart will be removed.

6. For pintucks in the center of the hearts - Cut a rectangle of fabric 12" by 6". Stitch double needle pintucks ¹/₄" apart parallel to the 12" side. This will make enough pintucked fabric for the sleeve hearts and the heart on the back of the blouse.

7. Place the pintucked fabric in the "hole" of the heart. Zigzag stitch around the inner edge of the lace heart. Stitch pintucked fabric in place along the inside edges of the lace. Remember to save enough pintucking for the hearts on the sleeves. Trim away any excess pintucked fabric from behind the lace.

Neck Finish

Refer to the general blouse directions II. Neck Finishes - B. Bias Binding found on page 17. A wing needle entredeux stitch can be place at the neck seam if desired.

Embellishing the Sleeve

Repeat the following directions for both sleeves.

1. Place two sleeve pieces right sides together at the top of the sleeves and stitch. Trace the three heart template in the center of each sleeve $2^3/_4$" from the end of the sleeve.

2. Shape the lace hearts using the techniques found in the heart lace shaping section on page 40. The two back hearts will be shaped first and the front heart will be shaped over the ends of the back hearts.

3. Stitch the back hearts on both sides of the lace using a zigzag or wing needle hem stitch. Using a zigzag or a wing needle hem stitch, stitch the front heart on the outer edge of the lace only.

4. Trim the fabric behind the lace of the back hearts.

5. Trim the fabric behind the lace of the front heart. The center fabric will be removed. Place pintucked fabric in the center of the heart as described in step 7 above - Embellishing the Blouse Front and Back.

6. Stitch three rows of pintucks $^1/_4$" apart starting $^1/_2$" above the bottom of the sleeve.

7. Run two gathering rows $^1/_4$" and $^1/_8$", between the marks in the top of the sleeve. Gather to fit the blouse front/back. Stitch in place.

8. Place a wing needle entredeux stitch along each seam for decoration, if desired.

9. Place one pintuck $^3/_8$" from the seam.

10. Cut two pieces of $^5/_8$" lace insertion 10" long. Center each piece along shoulder seam (5" in front, 5" in back) with one edge of the insertion along the sleeve seam. (Note: the lace will be placed over the pintuck). Fold the cut ends of the lace in a point. Pin in place and stitch using a zigzag or wing needle entredeux.

11. Cut two cuff pieces.

12. Along the top edge of each cuff, starting $^1/_2$" from the cut edge, stitch five double needle pintucks about $^1/_4$" apart. Fold the cuff in half, wrong sides together, and press. To finish the sleeves refer to the general directions III. Finishing the Sleeves - A. Cuff found on page 18. ✖

Camisole/Shell

Since the pattern piece is the same for the front and back, and is lined, this top can be worn back or front and can be reversible. When made in four colors this top adds versatility to a printed outfit or becomes a multi-purpose shell to compliment your current wardrobe. This shell may also be worn as a camisole underneath sheer or lace blouses. It is a must for any season.

Materials Required

Fabric - all sizes:

45"	1-3/4 yards
60"	7/8 yard

Lining:

45"	1-3/4 yards
60"	7/8 yard

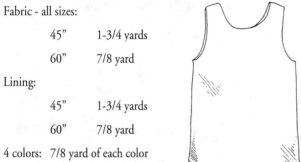

4 colors: 7/8 yard of each color
Notions: thread to match fabric
Pattern Pieces Needed: one piece used for front, back and lining.
Pattern pieces can be found on the pull-out.

A. Layout and Cutting

1. On the fold, cut one piece for the front, one piece for the back, and two pieces for the lining (**fig. 1 or fig. 1a**).

2. Stay stitch the neck edges.

B. Constructing the Garment

1. Place the front to the back, right sides together, at one side. Stitch, leaving one side stitched and one side open for the lining. Repeat for the lining (**fig. 2**).

2. Place the lining to the blouse, right sides together. Stitch along the neck edge, armscye, and the hem (**fig. 3**). This creates a tube.

3. Insert your hand in the tube and pull one side of the blouse into the other side of the blouse, placing raw edges and right sides of fabric together at the side seam. Stitch the two circles together with a 1/4" seam, leaving a 4" opening (**fig. 4**).

4. Before turning, insert your hand through the 4" slit and push the shoulder straps up into the lining shoulder straps. This makes a tube (**fig. 5**).

5. Stitch the two circles or tubes together with a 1/4" seam on both shoulders (**fig. 6**).

6. Turn the blouse through the 4" slit so that the seams are inside (**fig. 7**).

7. Stitch the 4" slit together by hand (**fig. 8**). Press.

8. Neck, armscyes and hem can be top stitched, if desired. ✂

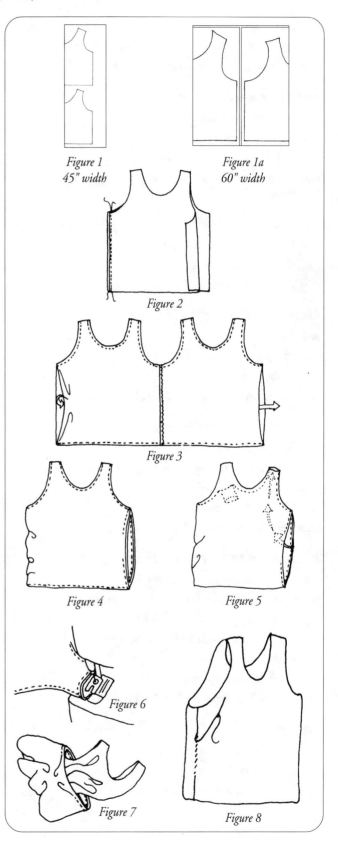

Figure 1
45" width

Figure 1a
60" width

Figure 2

Figure 3

Figure 4

Figure 5

Figure 6

Figure 7

Figure 8

Beginning French Sewing Techniques

Lace to Lace

Butt together and zigzag.

Suggested machine settings: Width $2^1/_2$, length 1.

Lace to Fabric

Place right sides together.

Fabric extends $^1/_8$" from lace.

Zigzag off the edge and over the heading of the lace.

Suggested Machine Settings: Width $3^1/_2$, Length $^1/_2$ to 1 (almost a satin stitch).

Lace to Entredeux

Trim batiste from one side of the entredeux.

Butt lace to entredeux and zigzag.

Suggested Machine Settings: Width $2^1/_2$, Length $1^1/_2$.

Gathered Lace to Entredeux

Trim one side of the entredeux.

Gather lace by pulling heading thread.

Butt together and zigzag.

Suggested Machine Settings: Width $2^1/_2$, Length $1^1/_2$.

Entredeux to Flat Fabric

Place fabric to entredeux, right sides together.

Stitch in the ditch with a regular straight stitch.

Trim seam allowance to $^1/_8$".

Zigzag over the seam allowance.

Suggested Machine Settings: Width $2^1/_2$, Length $1^1/_2$.

Entredeux to Gathered Fabric

Gather fabric using two gathering rows.

Place gathered fabric to entredeux, right sides together.

Stitch in the ditch with a regular straight stitch.

Stitch again $^1/_{16}$" away from the first stitching.

Trim seam allowance to $^1/_8$".

Zigzag over the seam allowance.

Suggested Machine Settings: Width $2^1/_2$, Length $1^1/_2$.

Top Stitch

Turn seam down, away from the lace, entredeux, etc.

Tack in place using a zigzag.

Suggested Machine Settings: Width $1^1/_2$, Length $1^1/_2$. ❁

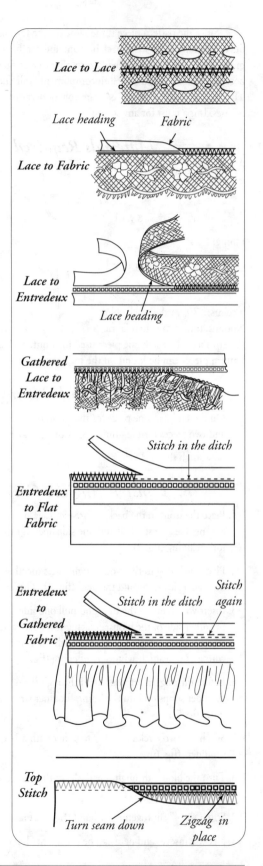

Lace to Lace

Lace heading   Fabric

Lace to Fabric

Lace to Entredeux

Lace heading

Gathered Lace to Entredeux

Stitch in the ditch

Entredeux to Flat Fabric

Stitch in the ditch   Stitch again

Entredeux to Gathered Fabric

Top Stitch

Turn seam down   Zigzag in place

*Pink Linen Heart/Bow
Embroidered Blouse*

*Singer Floral and
Hemstitched Fantasy*

*Pfaff Embroidered
Delicate Designs*

*Baby Lock Embroidered
Motif Blouse*

*Detail of Baby Lock
Embroidered
Motif Blouse*

*Detail of Singer Floral
and Hemstitched Fantasy*

*Detail of Pfaff Embroidered
Delicate Designs*

*Elna Embroidred Blouse
with Pleated Cuffs*

New Home Fabulous Flowers

Bernina Flowers and
Faux Smocked Trim

Viking Embroidred
Netting Lace

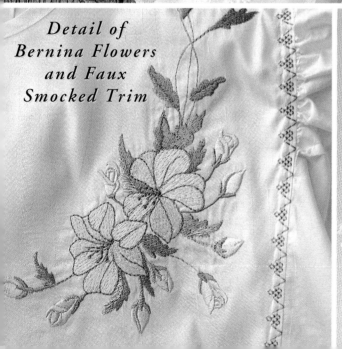

Detail of
Bernina Flowers
and Faux
Smocked Trim

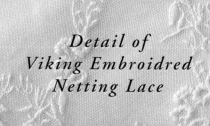

Detail of
Viking Embroidred
Netting Lace

Seminole Patchwork Blouse

Normandy Lace Silk
Dupioni Blouse

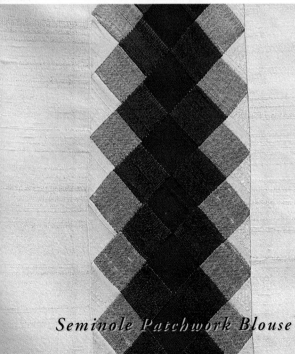

Seminole Patchwork Blouse

Normandy Lace Silk
Dupioni Blouse

Above Photograph

*Left: Ribbon and Organdy
        Sandwich Blouse*
Right: French Waterfall Blouse

Above Right Photograph

Spoke Collar Blouse

Right Photograph

Left: Wedding Blouse
*Right: Linen Transformation
         Blouse*

Lynne Holyoake
Puffing Blouse

Pink Linen
Heart/Bow
Embroidered Blouse

Cutwork Blouse

Shadow Shapes
Blouse

Detail of Cutwork Blouse

Cutting Fabric From Behind Lace That Has Been Shaped and Zigzagged

I absolutely love two pairs of Fiskars Scissors for the tricky job of cutting fabric from behind lace that has been shaped and stitched on. The first is Fiskars 9491, blunt tip 5" scissors. They look much like kindergarten scissors because of the blunt tips; however, they are very sharp. They cut fabric away from behind laces with ease. By the way, both of the scissors mentioned in this section are made for either right handed or left handed people.

The second pair that I really love for this task are the Fiskars 9808 curved blade craft scissors. The curved blades are very easy to use when working in tricky, small areas of lace shaping. Fiskars are crafted of permanent stainless steel and are precision ground and hardened for a sharp, long lasting edge.

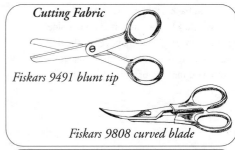

Cutting Fabric

Fiskars 9491 blunt tip

Fiskars 9808 curved blade

Repairing Lace Holes Which You Didn't Mean To Cut!

Trimming fabric away from behind stitched-down lace can be difficult. It is not uncommon to slip, thus cutting a hole in your lace work. How do you repair this lace with the least visible repair? It is really quite simple.

1. Look at the pattern in the lace where you have cut the hole. Is it in a flower, in a dot series, or in the netting part of the lace (**fig. 1**)?

2. After you identify the pattern where the hole was cut, cut another piece of lace ¹/₄" longer than each side of the hole in the lace.

3. On the bottom side of the lace in the garment, place the lace patch (**fig. 2**).

4. Match the design of the patch with the design of the lace around the hole where it was cut.

5. Zigzag around the cut edges of the lace hole, trying to catch the edges of the hole in your zigzag (**fig 3**).

6. Now, you have a patched and zigzagged pattern.

7. Trim away the leftover ends underneath the lace you have just patched (**fig. 3**).

8. And don't worry about a piece of patched lace. My grandmother used to say, "Don't worry about that. You'll never notice it on a galloping horse."

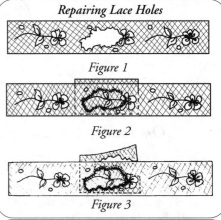

Repairing Lace Holes

Figure 1

Figure 2

Figure 3

Piecing Lace Not Long Enough For Your Needs

From my sewing experience, sometimes you will need a longer piece of lace than you have. Perhaps you cut the lace incorrectly or bought less than you needed and had to go back for more. Whatever the reason, if you need to make a lace strip longer, it is easy to do.

1. Match your pattern with two strips that will be joined later (**figs. 1 and 3**).

2. Is your pattern a definite flower? Is it a definite diamond or some other pattern that is relatively large?

3. If you have a definite design in the pattern, you can join pieces by zigzagging around that design and then down through the heading of the lace (**fig. 2**).

4. If your pattern is tiny, you can zigzag at an angle joining the two pieces (**fig. 2**). Trim away excess laces close to the zigzagged seam (**fig. 4**).

5. Forget that you have patched laces and complete the dress. If you discover that the lace is too short before you begin stitching, you can plan to place the pieced section in an inconspicuous place.

6. If you were already into making the garment when you discovered the short lace, simply join the laces and continue stitching as if nothing had happened.

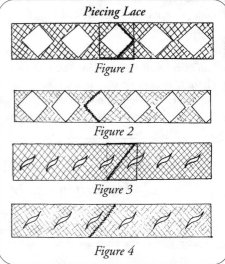

Piecing Lace

Figure 1

Figure 2

Figure 3

Figure 4

If Your Fancy Band Is Too Short

Not to worry; cut down the width of your skirt. Always make your skirt adapt to your lace shapes, not the lace shapes to your skirt.

Making Diamonds, Hearts, Tear-Drops, Or Circles Fit Skirt Bottom

How do you make sure that you engineer your diamonds, hearts, teardrops, or circles to exactly fit the width skirt that you are planning? The good news is that you don't. Make your shapes any size that you want. Stitch them onto your skirt, front and back, and cut away the excess skirt width. Or, you can stitch up one side seam, and zigzag your shapes onto the skirt, and cut away the excess on the other side before you make your other side seam. ✹

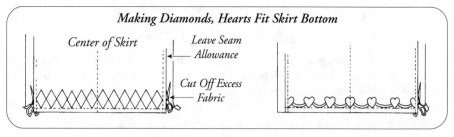

Making Diamonds, Hearts Fit Skirt Bottom

Center of Skirt — Leave Seam Allowance — Cut Off Excess Fabric

Machine Entredeux

Making Entredeux (Or Hemstitching) On Today's Computer Sewing Machines

About eight years ago I was conned into purchasing a 1905 hemstitching machine for $1500. I was told that it had a perfect stitch and that stitch (about 2 inches) was demonstrated to me by the traveling salesman. I was very happy to finally have one of those wonderful machines. Guess how long that wonderful machine lasted before it broke down? I stitched about 10 inches more which looked great; at that point, the stitching was awful. I called several repairmen. It never made a decent hemstitch again.

The good news to follow this sad story is that today's new computer machines do an excellent job of making hemstitching and they work! I am going to give our favorite settings for our favorite sewing machines. Before you buy a new sewing machine, if you love heirloom sewing, please go try out each of these machines and see if you love these stitches as much as we do.

Using A Stabilizer With Wing Needle Hemstitching Or Pinstitching

Before you do any hemstitching or any decorative work with a wing needle which involves lots of stitching on these wonderful machines, first let me tell you that **you must use a stabilizer**! You can use stitch-n-tear, computer paper, tissue paper (not quite strong enough but o.k. in certain situations), wax paper, physician's examining table paper, typing paper, adding machine paper or almost any other type of paper. When you are doing heavy stitching such as a feather stitch, I recommend that type of paper which physicians spread out over their examining tables. You can get a roll of it at any medical supply place. If you use stitch-n-tear or adding machine paper in feather stitch type stitches, it is difficult to pull away all of the little pieces which remain when you take the paper from the back of the garment. This physician's paper seems to tear away pretty easily.

Preparing Fabric Before Beginning Hemstitching or Pinstitching

Stiffen fabric with spray starch before lace shaping or decorative stitching with the hemstitches and wing needles. Use a hair dryer to dry the lace before you iron it if you have spray starched it too much. Also, if you wet your fabrics and laces too much with spray starch, place a piece of tissue paper on top of your work, and dry iron it dry. Hemstitching works best on natural fibers such as linen, cotton, cotton batiste, silk or cotton organdy. I don't advise

hemstitching a fabric with a high polyester content. Polyester has a memory. If you punch a hole in polyester, it remembers the original positioning of the fibers, and the hole wants to close up.

Threads To Use For Pinstitching Or Hemstitching

Use all cotton thread, 50, 60, 70, 80 weight. If you have a thread breaking problem, you can also use a high quality polyester thread or a cotton covered polyester thread, like the Coats and Clark for machine lingerie and embroidery. Personally, I like to press needle down on all of the entredeux and pin stitch settings.

Pinstitching Or Point de Paris Stitch With A Sewing Machine

The pin stitch is another lovely "entredeux look" on my favorite machines. It is a little more delicate. Pin stitch looks similar to a ladder with **one of the long sides of the ladder missing**. Imagine the steps being fingers which reach over into the actual lace piece to grab the lace. The side of the ladder, the long side, will be stitched on the fabric right along side of the outside of the heading of the lace. The fingers reach into the lace to grab it. You need to look on all of the pinstitch settings given below and realize that you have to use reverse image on one of the sides of lace so that the fingers will grab into the lace while the straight side goes on the outside of the lace heading.

Pfaff 7570

Pinstitch
  -100 wing needle, A - 2 Foot, Needle Down
  -Stitch 112, tension 3, twin needle button, 4.0 width, 3.0 length

Entredeux
  -100 wing needle, A - 2 Foot, Needle Down

	width	length
Stitch #132	3.5	5.0
Stitch #113	4.0	2.0
Stitch #114	3.5	2.5
Stitch #115	3.5	3.0

Bernina 1630

Pinstitch
  - 100 wing needle
  - 1630 menu G, Pattern #10, SW - 2.5, SL - 2

Entredeux
  - 100 wing needle
  - 1630 menu G, pattern #5, SW - 3.5, SL - 3

Viking #1+

Pinstitch
  - 100 wing needle
  -Stitch D6, width 2.5-3; length 2.5-3

Entredeux
  - 100 wing needle
  -Stitch D7 (width and length are already set in)

Elna 9000 and DIVA

Pinstitch
  - 100 wing needle
  -Stitch #120 (length and width are already set in)

Entredeux
  - 100 wing needle
  -Stitch #121 (length and width are already set)

Singer XL - 100

Pinstitch
  - 100 Wing Needle
  - Screen #3
  - Stitch #7
  - Width 4 (length changes with width)

Entredeux
  - 100 Wing needle
  - Screen #3
  - Stitch #8
  Width 5 (Medium) or 4 (small)

New Home 9000

Pinstitch
  - 100 Wing Needle
  - Stitch #26 (width 2.5; length 2.5)

Hemstitch
  - 100 wing needle
  - Stitch #39 (width 4.0; length 1.5)

Esanté - Baby Lock

Choose Decorative Stitch-Heirloom

Pinstitch
  - 100 wing needle
  - Stitch #4

Hemstitch
  - 100 wing needle
  - Stitch #5

Attaching Shaped Lace To The Garment With Machine Entredeux Or Pinstitching And A Wing Needle

Probably my favorite place to use the machine entredeux/wing needle hemstitching is to attach shaped laces to a garment. Simply shape your laces in the desired shapes such as hearts, diamonds, ovals, loops, circles, or bows, and stitch the stitch. In addition to stitching this gorgeous decorative stitch, it also attaches the shaped lace to the garment (**fig. 1**). Always use stabilizer when using this type of heavy hemstitching. ⊛

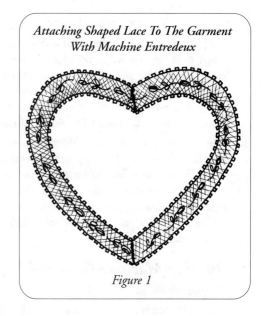

Attaching Shaped Lace To The Garment With Machine Entredeux

Figure 1

Puffing

Gathering The Puffing Using The Gathering Foot On Your Machine

Two years ago, I wouldn't have told you that this was the easiest method of applying puffing into a round portrait collar. The reason being I didn't know how to make perfect puffing using the gathering foot for the sewing machine. I thought you used the edge of the gathering foot to guide the fabric underneath the gathering foot. This left about a 1/4" seam allowance. It also made the gathers not perfect in some places with little "humps" and unevenness on some portions. Therefore, I wasn't happy with puffing made on the gathering foot. When I asked my friend, Sue Hausman, what might be wrong, she explained to me that to make perfect gathering, you had to move the fabric over so that you would have at least a 1/2" seam allowance. She further explained that there are two sides to the feed dogs; when you use the side of the gathering foot, then the fabric only catches on one side of the feed dogs. It works like magic to move your fabric over and guide it along one of the guide lines on the sewing machine. If your machine doesn't have these lines, simply put a piece of tape down to make a proper guide line.

Making Gathering Foot Puffing

1. The speed of the sewing needs to be consistent. Sew either fast or slow but do not sew fast then slow then fast again. For the beginner, touch the "sew slow" button (if available on your machine). This will help to keep a constant speed.

2. The puffing strip should be gathered with a 1/2 seam allowance, with an approximate straight stitch length of 4, right side up (**fig. 1**). Remember that you can adjust your stitch length to make your puffing looser or fuller. Do not let the strings of the fabric wrap around the foot of the machine. This will cause to fabric to back up behind the foot causing an uneven seam allowance, as well as uneven gathers. Leave the thread tails long in case adjustments are needed. One side of the gathering is now complete (**fig. 2**).

3. Begin gathering the second side of the strip, right side up. This row of gathering will be made from the bottom of the strip to the top of the strip. In other words, bi-directional sewing (first side sewn from the top to the bottom, second side sewn from the bottom to the top) is allowed. Gently unfold the ruffle with the left hand allowing flat fabric to feed under the foot. **Do not** apply any pressure to the fabric (**fig. 3**). The feeding must remain constant. Leave the thread tails long in case adjustments are needed. The puffing strip in now complete.

Placing Machine Gathered Puffing Into A Collar

1. Cut your strips of fabric.

2. Gather both sides of the puffing, running the fabric under the gathering foot. Be sure you have at least a 1/2" seam allowance. When you use a gathering foot, the moveability of the puffing isn't as great as when you gather it the other way.

3. You, of course, have two raw edges when you gather puffing with the gathering foot (**fig. 1**).

4. Shape the puffing around the fabric board below the row of lace (or rows of lace) that you have already shaped into the rounded shape. Place the pins into the board through the outside edge of the puffing. Place the pins right into the place where the gathering row runs in the fabric (**fig. 2**).

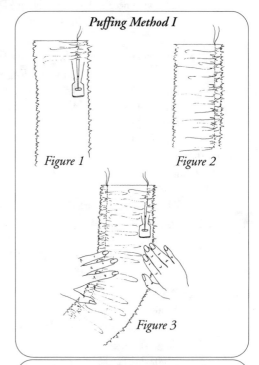

Puffing Method I

Figure 1   Figure 2

Figure 3

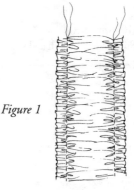

Placing Machine Gathered Puffing Into A Collar

Figure 1

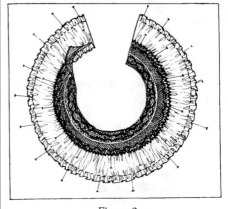

Figure 2

5. Pull the raw edge of the machine puffed strip up **underneath the finished edge of the curved lace**, so that your zigzagging to attach the puffing will be on the machine gathering line. Put the rounded lace edge on top of the puffing. Pin the bottom edge of the puffing first so you can "arrange" the top fullness underneath the curved lace edge which is already in place (the top piece of lace) (**see fig. 2**).

6. It will be necessary to "sort of" arrange the machine gathered puffing, especially on the top edge which will be gathered the fullest on your collar, and pin it where you want it since the machine gathering thread doesn't give too much. After you have pinned and poked the gathering into place where it looks pretty on the top and the bottom, flat pin it to the tissue paper and zigzag the puffing strip to the lace, stitching right on top of the lace.

NOTE: **You will have an unfinished fabric edge underneath the place where you stitched the lace to the puffing.** That is okay. After you have zigzagged the puffing to the lace, then trim away the excess fabric underneath the lace edge. Be careful, of course, when you trim this excess fabric, not to accidentally cut the lace.

7. If you have a machine entredeux/wing needle option on your sewing machine, you can stitch this beautiful stitch in place of the zigzagging. Since the fabric is gathered underneath the lace, you will have to be very careful stitching to get a pretty stitch.

8. Shape another piece of lace around the bottom of this puffing, bringing the inside piece of curved lace exactly to fit on top of the gathering line in the puffing. Once again, you will have unfinished fabric underneath the place where you will zigzag the lace to the puffing collar. After zigzagging the lace to the puffing collar, trim the excess fabric away.

9. Continue curving the rest of the laces to make the collar as wide as you want it to be. ✾

Basic Pintucking

Double Needles

Double needles come in different sizes. The first number on the double needle is the distance between the needles. The second number on the needle is the actual size of the needle. The chart below shows some of the double needle sizes. The size needle that you choose will depend on the weight of the fabric that you are pintucking (**fig. 1**).

Let me relate a little more information for any of you who haven't used the double needles yet. Some people have said to me, "Martha, I only have a place for one needle in my sewing machine." That is correct and on most sewing machines, you probably still can use a double needle. The double needle has only one stem which goes into the needle slot; the double needles join on a little bar below the needle slot. You use two spools of thread when you thread the double needles. If you don't have two spools of thread of the fine thread which you use for pintucking, then run an extra bobbin and use it as another spool of thread. For most shaped pintucking on heirloom garments, I prefer either the 1.6/70, the 1.6/80 or the 2.0/80 size needle.

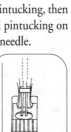

Figure 1

a. 1.6/70 - Light Weight
b. 1.6/80 - Light Weight
c. 2.0/80 - Light Weight
d. 2.5/80 - Light Weight
e. 3.0/90 - Medium Weight
f. 4.0/100 - Heavy Weight

Figure 2

Pintuck Feet

Pintuck feet are easy to use and they shave hours off pintucking time when you are making straight pintucks. They enable you to space straight pintucks perfectly. I might add here that some people also prefer a pintuck foot when making curved and angled pintucks. I prefer a regular zigzag sewing foot for curved pintucks. Pintuck feet correspond to the needle used with that pintuck foot; the needle used corresponds to the weight of fabric. The bottom of these feet have a certain number of grooves 3, 5, 7, or 9. The width of the groove matches the width between the two needles. When making straight pintucks, use a pintuck foot of your choice. The grooves enable one to make those pintucks as close or as far away as the distance on the foot allows (**fig. 2**).

Preparing Fabric For Pintucking

Do I spray starch the fabric before I pintuck it? I usually do not spray starch fabric before pintucking it. Always press all-cotton fabric. A polyester/cotton blend won't need to be pressed unless it is very wrinkled. Tucks tend to lay flatter if you stiffen fabric with spray starch first; that is why I don't advise spray starching the fabric first in most cases. Pintuck a small piece of your chosen fabric with starch and one without starch, then make your own decision.

Straight Pintucking With A Pintuck Foot

Some of my favorite places for straight pintucks are on high yoke bodices of a dress and along the sleeves. On ladies blouses, straight pintucks are lovely running vertically on the front and back of the blouse, and so slenderizing! One of the prettiest treatments of straight pintucks on ladies blouses is stitching about three to five pintucks right down the center back of the blouse. Tuck a little shaped bow or heart on the center back of the blouse; stitch several tiny pintucks and top them off with a lace shape in the center back. Horizontally placed straight pintucks are lovely running across the back yoke of a tailored blouse. Tucks are always pretty running around the cuff of a blouse. I love pintucks just about anywhere.

1. Put in your double needle. Thread machine with two spools of thread. Thread one spool at a time (including the needle). This will help keep the threads from becoming twisted while stitching the tucks. This would be a good time to look in the guide book which came with your sewing machine for directions on using pintuck feet and double needles. Some sewing machines have a special way of threading for use with double needles.

2. The first tuck must be straight. To make this first tuck straight, do one of three things: (**a.**) Pull a thread all the way across the fabric and follow along that pulled line. (**b.**) Using a measuring stick, mark a straight line along the fabric. Stitch on that line. (**c.**) Fold the fabric in half and press that fold. Stitch along that folded line.

3. Place the fabric under the foot for the first tuck and straight stitch the desired length of pintuck. (Length=1 to $2^1/_2$; Needle position is center) (**fig. 1**).

4. Place your first tuck into one of the grooves in your pintuck foot. The space between each pintuck depends on the placement of the first pintuck (**fig. 2**).

5. Continue pintucking by placing the last pintuck made into a groove in the foot.

Straight Pintucking Without A Pintuck Foot

1. Use a double needle. Use your regular zigzag foot.

2. Thread your double needles.

3. Draw the first line of pintucking. Pintuck along that line. At this point you can use the edge of your presser foot as a guide (**fig. 3**).

NOTE: You might find a "generic" pintuck foot for your particular brand of machine.

Corded Pintucks

Cords make pintucks more prominent. Use Mettler gimp or #8 pearl cotton. Cording comes in handy when pintucks are being shaped. When pintucking across a bias with a double needle, you may get some distortion. The cord acts as a filler and will keep the fabric from distorting. Sometimes you might choose to use cording in order to add color to your pintucks. If you asked me, "Martha, do you usually cord pintucks?," my answer would be "no." However, just because I don't usually cord pintucks, doesn't mean that you won't prefer to cord them.

Some machines have a little device which sits in the base of the machine and sticks up just a little bit. That device tends to make the pintucks stand up a little more for a higher raised effect. Some people really like this feature.

1. If your machine has a hole in the throat plate, run the cord up through that hole and it will be properly placed without another thought (**fig. 2**).

2. If your machine does not have a hole in the throat plate, put the gimp or pearl cotton underneath the fabric, lining it up with the pintuck groove. Once you get the cording lined up under the proper groove, it will follow along for the whole pintuck.

3. You can stitch pintucks without a pintuck foot at all. Some sewing machines have a foot with a little hole right in the middle of the foot underneath the foot. That is a perfectly proper place to place the cord for shadow pintucks. Remember, if you use a regular foot for pintucking, you must use the side of the foot for guiding your next pintuck.

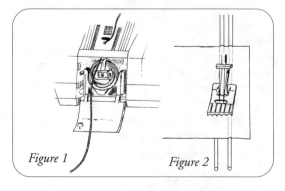

Figure 1   *Figure 2*

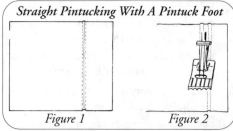

Straight Pintucking With A Pintuck Foot

Figure 1   *Figure 2*

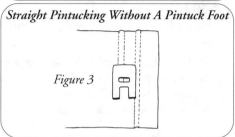

Straight Pintucking Without A Pintuck Foot

Figure 3

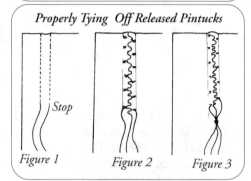

Properly Tying Off Released Pintucks

Stop

Figure 1   *Figure 2*   *Figure 3*

Shaping Curves And Angles With Pintucks

Pintucks are inexpensive to make. They add texture and dimension without adding cost to the dress. They're rarely found on store-bought clothing. One of my favorite things in the whole world to do is to follow lace shapes with pintucks or decorative stitches on your machine for an enchanting finish. Or you may simply use your template and pintuck the shape instead of using lace. For threads, use white-on-white, ecru-on-ecru, or any pastel color on white or ecru.

The effect of shaped pintucks is so fabulous and so interesting. Virtually everybody is afraid that she doesn't know how to make those fabulous pintucks that transform a garment into a pintuck fantasy. It is so easy that I just can't wait to share with you the tricks. I promise, nobody in my schools all over the world ever believes me when I tell them this easiest way. Then, everybody, virtually everybody, has done these curved and angled pintucks with absolute perfection. They usually say, "This is really magic!"

The big question here is, "What foot do I use for scalloped pintucks?" For straight pintucks, I use a pintuck foot with the grooves. That foot is fine for curved or scalloped pintucks also, but I prefer either the regular zigzag foot or the clear appliqué foot, which is plastic and allows easy "see through" of the turning points. Try your pintuck foot, your regular sewing foot, and your clear appliqué foot to see which one you like the best. Like all aspects of heirloom sewing, the "best" foot is really your personal preference. Listed below are my absolute recommendations for curved and angled pintucks.

Martha's General Rules Of Curving And Angling Pintucks

1. Use a regular zigzag foot, or a pintuck foot (**fig. 1**).

2. Either draw on your pintuck shape, or zigzag your lace insertion to the garment. You can either draw on pintuck shapes or follow your lace shaping. My favorite way to make lots of pintucks is to follow lace shaping which has already been stitched to the garment.

3. Using a ruler, draw straight lines with a fabric marker or washable pencil, bisecting each point where you will have to turn around with your pintuck. In other words, draw a line at all angles where you will have to turn your pintuck in order to keep stitching. This is the most important point to make with curved and angled pintucks. When you are going around curves, this bi-secting line is not necessary since you don't stop and pivot when you are turning curves. Everywhere you have to stop and pivot, these straight lines must be drawn (**fig. 2**).

4. Use a 1.6 or a 2.0 double needle. Any wider doesn't curve or turn well!

5. Set your machine for straight sewing, L=1.5. Notice this is a **very short stitch**. When you turn angles, this short stitch is necessary for pretty turns.

6. Press "Needle Down" on your sewing machine if your machine has this feature. This means that when you stop sewing at any time, your needle will remain in the fabric.

7. Stitch, using either the first line you drew or following around the lace shaping which you have already stitched to your garment. The edge of your presser foot will guide along the outside of the lace shape. When you go around curves, turn your fabric and keep stitching. Do not pick up your foot and pivot, this makes the curves jumpy, not smooth (**fig. 3**).

8. When you come to a pivot point, let your foot continue to travel until you can look into the hole of the foot, and see that your double needles have **straddled the line you drew on the fabric.** Remember your needles are **in the fabric** (**fig. 4**).

9. Sometimes, the needles won't exactly straddle the line exactly the way they straddled the line on the last turn around. Lift the presser foot. (Remember, you needles are still in the fabric.) Turn your fabric where the edge of the presser foot properly begins in a new direction following your lace insertion lace shaping or your drawn line, lower the presser foot, and begin sewing again (**fig. 5**).

10. Wait A Minute! Most of you are now thinking, "Martha, You Are Crazy. There are two major problems with what you just said. You said to leave the double needles in the fabric, lift the presser foot , turn the fabric, lower the presser foot and begin sewing again. If I do that I will probably break my double needles, and there will be a big wad or hump of fabric where I twisted the fabric to turn around to go in a new direction. That will never work!" I know you are thinking these two things because everybody does. Neither one of these things will happen! It is really just like MAGIC. TRY THIS TECHNIQUE AND SEE WHAT I AM SAYING. Ladies all over the world absolutely adore this method and nobody believes how easy it is.

11. After you get your first row of double needle pintucks, then you can use the edge of your regular zigzag sewing machine foot, guiding along the just stitched pintuck row as the guide point for more rows. The only thing you have to remember, is to make long enough lines to bisect each angle that you are going to turn. You must have these turn-around lines drawn so you can know where to stop sewing, leave the needles in the fabric, turn around, and begin stitching again. These lines are the real key. ❂

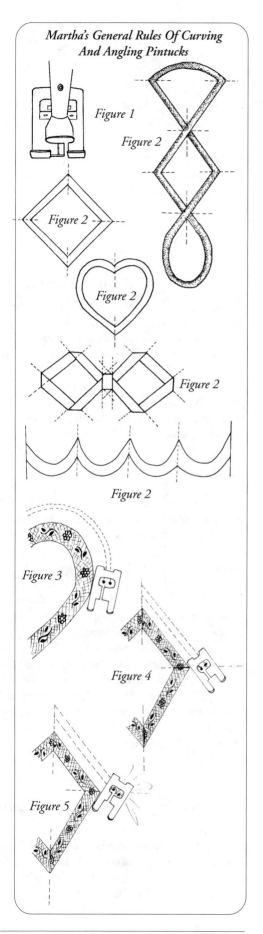

Martha's General Rules Of Curving And Angling Pintucks

Figure 1

Figure 2

Figure 2

Figure 2

Figure 2

Figure 2

Figure 3

Figure 4

Figure 5

Lace Shaping Techniques

General Lace Shaping Supplies

- ❁ Fabric to apply lace shape
- ❁ Lace (usually insertion lace)
- ❁ Glass head pins
- ❁ Spray starch
- ❁ Lightweight sewing thread
- ❁ Lace shaping board or covered cardboard
- ❁ Washout marker or washout pencil
- ❁ Wing needle (optional)
- ❁ Stabilizer (If a wing needle stitch is used)

Using Glass Head Pins

Purchasing GLASS HEAD PINS is one of the first and most critical steps to lace shaping. All types of lace shaping must be pinned in place, starched lightly and pressed. The iron is placed directly on top of the pins. Since plastic head pins melt onto your fabric and ruin your project, obviously they won't do. Metal pins such as the iris pins with the skinny little metal heads won't melt; however, when you pin hundreds of these little pins into the lace shaping board, your finger will have one heck of a hole poked into it. Please purchase glass head pins and throw away your plastic head pins. Glass head pins can be purchased by the box or by the card. For dress projects, as many 100 pins might be needed for each section of lace shaping. So, make sure to purchase enough.

Shape 'N Press (Lace Shaping Board)

I used fabric boards (covered cardboard) until the June Taylor's Shape 'N Press board became available. It is truly wonderful. This board measures 24" by 18" and has permanent lace shaping templates drawn right on the board. I never have to hunt for another lace shaping template again. Here is how I use it. I place my skirt, collar, pillow top or other project on top of the board with the desired template positioned correctly (I can see the template through the fabric), shape the lace along the template lines pinning into the board, spray starch lightly, re-pin the lace just to the fabric. Now I can move the fabric, correctly positioning the template, and start the process again. Did you notice, I never mentioned tracing the design on the fabric? With the Shape 'N Press, drawing on the fabric can be omitted so you never have to worry about removing fabric marker lines. I also use the flip side of the board. It has a blocking guide for bishops and round collars (sizes newborn to adult).

Shape 'N Press Board

Making A Lace Shaping Board or Fabric Board

If a lace shaping board is not available, a fabric board can be made from cardboard (cake boards, pizza boards or a cut up box) covered with fabric or paper. A child's bulletin board or a fabric covered ceiling tile will work. Just staple or pin fabric or white typing paper or butcher paper over the board before you begin lace shaping. Just remember you must be able to pin into the board, use a bit of stray starch and iron on it.

Tracing the Template

Trace the template on the fabric with a wash out marker. Margaret Boyles taught me years ago that it is simpler to draw your shapes on fabric by making dots about one half inch apart than it is to draw a solid line. This also means less pencil or marker to get out of the fabric when your lace shaping is finished. Mark

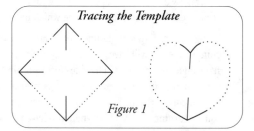

Tracing the Template

Figure 1

all angles with miter lines (a line dividing the angle in half). Sometimes it is helpful to make the solid lines at the angles and miter lines (**fig. 1**). Hint: If you do not want to draw the template on the fabric, trace the template on stabilizer or paper with a permanent marker. Place the template under the fabric. Because the fabric is "see-through" the lines can be seen clearly. Shape the lace along the template lines. Complete the design as stated in the lace shaping directions. Remember to remove the template paper before stitching so that the permanent pen lines are not caught in the stitching.

Shish Kabob Sticks

I first learned about using wooden shish kabob sticks from some of the technical school sewing teachers in Australia. By the way, where does one get these wooden shish kabob sticks? At the grocery store! If you can only find the long ones, just break them in half to measure 5" or 6" long and use the end with the point to push and to hold laces (or other items) as they go into the sewing machine. These sticks are used instead of the usual long pin or worse still, seam ripper that I have used so often. Using this stick is a safety technique as well as an efficient technique. ❁

Shaping Lace Diamonds

Lace diamonds can be used almost anywhere on heirloom garments. They are especially pretty at the point of a collar, on the skirt of a dress, at angles on the bodice of a garment, or all the way around a collar. The easiest way to make lace diamonds is to work on a fabric board with a diamond guide. You can make your diamonds as large or as small as you desire. I think you are really going to love this easy method of making diamonds with the fold back miter. Now, you don't have to remove those diamonds from the board to have perfect diamonds every time.

Making Lace Diamonds

Materials Needed
- ❋ Spray starch, iron, pins, fabric board
- ❋ Lace insertion
- ❋ Diamond guide

1. Draw the diamond guide or template (**fig. 1**).

2. Tear both skirt pieces. French seam or serge one side only of the skirt.

3. Working from the center seam you just made, draw diamonds all the way around the skirt. This way you can make any sized diamonds you want without worrying if they will fit the skirt perfectly. When you get all the way around both sides of the skirt you will have the same amount of skirt left over on both sides.

4. Simply trim the excess skirt away. Later you will French seam or serge the skirt on the other side to complete your skirt. This is the easy way to make any type of lace shaping on any skirt and it will always fit perfectly (**fig. 2**).

5. The guide or template, which you have just drawn, will be the outside of the diamond. Draw lines going into the diamond, bisecting each angle where the lace will be mitered. This is very important, since one of your critical pins will be placed exactly on this line. These bisecting lines need to be drawn about 2 inches long coming in from the angles of the diamonds (**fig. 3**). If you are making a diamond skirt, it is easier to draw your diamond larger and make your diamond shaping on the inside of the diamond. That way, the outside points of your diamond can touch when you are drawing all of your diamonds on the skirt.

6. As I said earlier, you can shape the laces for diamonds on either the outside or the inside of the template. I actually think it is easier to shape your laces on the inside of the template.

7. Place your skirt with the drawn diamonds on a fabric board.

8. Place the lace flat and guiding it along the inside of the drawn template, put a pin at **point A** and one at **point B** where the bisecting line goes to the inside (**fig. 4a**). The pin goes through both the lace and the fabric into the fabric board.

9. Guiding the edge of the lace along the drawn template line, place another pin into the fabric board through the lace (and the fabric skirt) at **point C** and another one at **point D** on the bisecting line (**fig. 4b**).

10. Fold back the lace right on top of itself. Remove the pin from the fabric board at **point D**, replacing it this time to go through both layers of lace rather than just one. Of course, the pin will not only go through both layers of lace but also through the skirt and into fabric board (**fig. 5**).

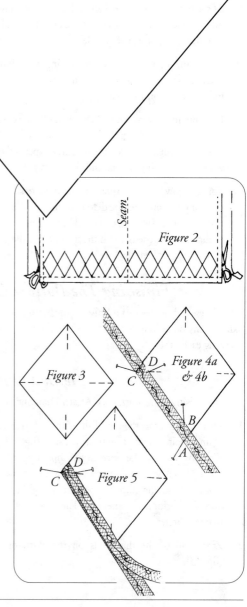

Figure 1

Seam

Figure 2

Figure 3

Figure 4a & 4b

Figure 5

11. Take the lace piece and bring it around to once again follow the outside line. You magically have a folded miter already in place (**see fig. 6**).

12. Guiding further, with the edge of the lace along the inside of the drawn template line, place another pin into the fabric board through the lace at **point E** and another at **point F** on the bisecting line (**fig. 6**).

13. Fold the lace right back on top of itself. Remove the pin at **point F**, replacing it this time to go through both layers of lace rather than just one (**fig. 7**).

14. Take the lace piece and bring it around to once again follow the outside line. You magically have a folded miter already in place (**fig. 8**).

15. Guiding further, with the edge of the lace along the inside of the drawn template line, place another pin into the lace at **point G** and another pin at **point H** on the bisecting line.

16. Fold the lace right back on top of itself. Remove the pin at **point H**, replace it this time to go through both layers of lace rather than just one.

17. Take the lace piece and bring it around to once again follow the outside line. You magically have a folded miter already in place (**fig. 9**).

18. At the bottom of the lace diamond, let the laces cross at the bottom. Remove the pin at **point B** and replace it into the fabric board through both pieces of lace. Remove the pin completely at **point A** (**fig. 10**).

19. Taking the top piece of lace, and leaving in the pin at **point B** only, fold the lace under and back so that it lies on top of the other piece of lace. You now have a folded in miter for the bottom of the lace.

20. Put a pin in, now, at **point B** (**fig. 11**). Of course you are going to have to cut away this long tail of lace. I think the best time to do that is before you begin your final stitching to attach the diamonds to the garment. It is perfectly alright to leave those tails of lace until your final stitching is done and then trim them.

21. You are now ready to spray starch and press the whole diamond shape. After spray starching and pressing the diamonds to the skirt, remove the pins from the fabric board and flat pin the lace shape to the skirt bottom. You are now ready to zigzag the diamond or machine entredeux stitch the diamond to the garment. Suggested zigzag settings are Width=2 to 3, Length=1 to 1¹/₂.

Finishing The Bottom Of The Skirt

These techniques are for finishing the bottom of a Diamond Skirt, a Heart Skirt, a Bow Skirt, or any other lace shaped skirt where the figures travel all the way around the bottom touching each other.

Method One

Using Plain Zigzag To Attach Diamonds (Or Other Shapes) To The Skirt

1. First, zigzag across the top of the diamond pattern, stitching from **point A** to **point B**, again to **point A** and finish the entire skirt (**fig. 12**). Your lace is now attached to the skirt all the way across the skirt on the top. If your fabric and diamonds have been spray starched well, you don't have to use a stabilizer when zigzagging these lace shapes to the fabric. The stitch width will be wide enough to cover the heading of the lace and go off onto the fabric on the other side. The length will be from ¹/₂ to 1, depending on the look that you prefer.

2. Zigzag all of the diamonds on the skirt, on the inside of the diamonds only (**fig. 13**).

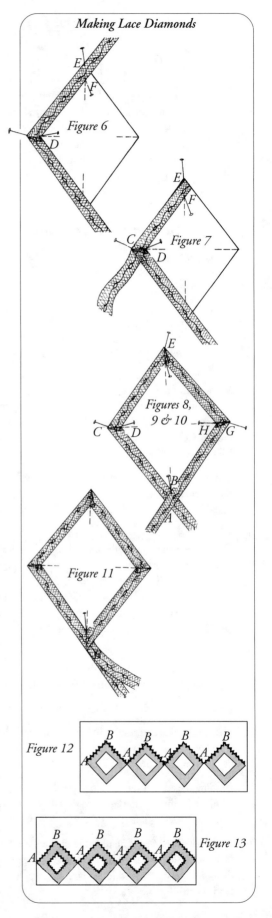

Making Lace Diamonds

Figure 6

Figure 7

Figures 8, 9 & 10

Figure 11

Figure 12

Figure 13

3. You are now ready to trim away the fabric of the skirt from behind the diamonds. Trim the fabric carefully from behind the lace shapes. The rest of the skirt fabric will now fall away leaving a diamond shaped bottom of the skirt (**fig. 14**). The lace will also be seen through the top of the diamonds.

4. If you are going to just gather lace and attach it at this point, then gather the lace and zigzag it to the bottom of the lace shapes, being careful to put extra fullness in the points of the diamonds (**fig. 15**). If your lace isn't wide enough to be pretty, then zigzag a couple of pieces of insertion or edging to your edging to make it wider (**fig. 16**).

5. If you are going to put entredeux on the bottom of the shapes before attaching gathered lace to finish it, follow the instructions for attaching entredeux to the bottom of a scalloped skirt given earlier in this lace shaping section. Work with short pieces of entredeux stitching from the inside points of the diamonds to the lower points of the diamonds on the skirt.

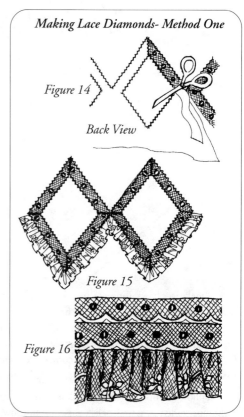

Making Lace Diamonds- Method One

Figure 14

Back View

Figure 15

Figure 16

Finishing The Bottom Of The Skirt
Method Two

Using A Wing Needle Machine Entredeux Stitch To Attach Diamonds
(Or Other Lace Shapes) To The Skirt

1. If you are going to use the wing needle/entredeux stitch on your sewing machine to attach your diamonds or other lace shapes to the skirt, use the entredeux stitch for all attaching of the lace shapes to the skirt. Remember **you must use a stabilizer** when using the entredeux stitch/wing needle on any machine.

2. Place your stabilizer underneath the skirt, behind the shapes to be stitched. You can use small pieces of stabilizer which are placed underneath only a few shapes rather than having to have a long piece of stabilizer. Just be sure that you have stabilizer underneath these lace shapes before you begin your entredeux/wing needle stitching.

3. First, stitch the top side of the diamonds entredeux stitching from point A to point B all the way around the skirt. (**fig. 17**).

4. Secondly, stitch the inside of the diamonds using the entredeux stitch (**fig. 18**). Do not cut any fabric away at this point. Remember to continue using stabilizer for all entredeux/wing needle stitching.

5. You are now ready to gather your lace edging and machine entredeux it to the bottom of the skirt, joining the bottom portions of the diamonds at the same time you attach the gathered lace edging. If your machine has an edge joining or edge stitching foot with a center blade for guiding, this is a great place for using it.

6. Gather only a few inches of lace edging at a time. Butt the gathered lace edging to the flat bottom sides of the diamonds.

7. Machine entredeux right between the gathered lace edging and the flat side of the diamond. Remember, you are stitching through your laces (which are butted together, not overlapped), the fabric of the skirt and the stabilizer (**fig. 19**). Put a little extra lace gathered fullness at the upper and lower points of the diamonds.

8. After you have stitched your machine entredeux all the way around the bottom of the skirt, you have attached the gathered lace edging to the bottom of the skirt with your entredeux stitch.

9. Trim the fabric from behind the lace diamonds. Trim the fabric from underneath the gathered lace edging on the bottom of the skirt (**fig. 20**).

10. Either zigzag your folded miters in the angles of the diamonds or simply leave them folded in. I prefer to zigzag them (**fig. 21**). You also have the choice of cutting away the little folded back portions of the miters or leaving them for strength. ⊛

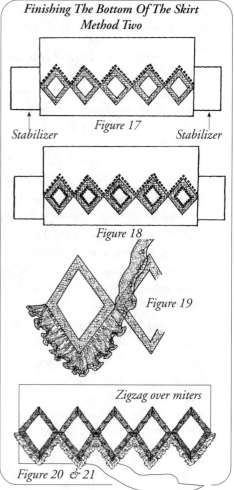

Finishing The Bottom Of The Skirt
Method Two

Stabilizer *Figure 17* *Stabilizer*

Figure 18

Figure 19

Zigzag over miters

Figure 20 & 21

Shaping Flip-Flopped Lace Bows

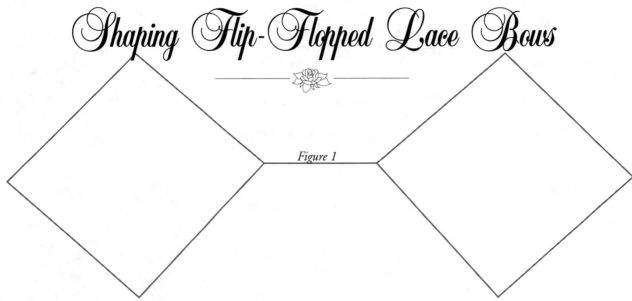

Figure 1

I make lace bows using a technique called "flip-flopping" lace — a relatively unsophisticated name for such a lovely trim. I first saw this technique on an antique teddy I bought at a local antique store. It had the most elegant flip-flopped lace bow. Upon careful examination, I noticed the lace was simply folded over at the corners, then continued down forming the outline of the bow. The corners were somewhat square. Certainly it was easier than mitering or pulling a thread and curving. I found it not only looked easier, it was easier.

Follow the instructions for making a flip-flopped bow, using a bow template. This technique works just as well for lace angles up and down on a skirt. You can flip-flop any angle that traditionally would be mitered. It can be used to go around a square collar, around diamonds, and around any shape with an angle rather than a curve.

Flip-Flopping Lace

1. Trace the template onto the fabric exactly where you want to place bows (**fig. 1**). Remember, the easy way to put bows around a skirt is to fold the fabric to make equal divisions of the skirt. If you want a bow skirt which has bows all the way around, follow the directions for starting at the side to make the bows in the directions given for a diamond skirt.

2. Draw your bows on your garment or on a skirt where you want this lace shape.

3. Place your garment on your fabric board before you begin making your bow shapes. Beginning above the inside of one bow (**above E**), place the lace along the angle. The template is the inside guide line of the bow (**fig. 2**).

4. At the first angle (**B**), simply fold the lace so that it will follow along the next line (**B-C**) (**fig. 3**). This is called flip-flopping the lace.

5. Place pins sticking through the lace, the fabric, and into the shaping board. I like to place pins on both the inside edges and the outside edges. Remember to place your pins so that they lie as flat as possible.

6. The lines go as follows: A-B, B-C, C-D, D-A, E-F, F-G, G-H, H-E. Tuck your lace end under E, which is also where the first raw edge will end (**fig. 4**).

7. Cut a short bow tab of lace that is long enough to go around the whole tie area of the bow (**fig. 4**). This will be the bow tie!

8. Tuck in this lace tab to make the center of the bow (**fig. 5**). Another way to attach this bow tie is to simply fold down a tab at the top and the bottom and place it right on top of the center of the bow. That is actually easier than tucking it under. Since you are going to zigzag all the way around the bow "tie" it really won't matter whether it is tucked in or not.

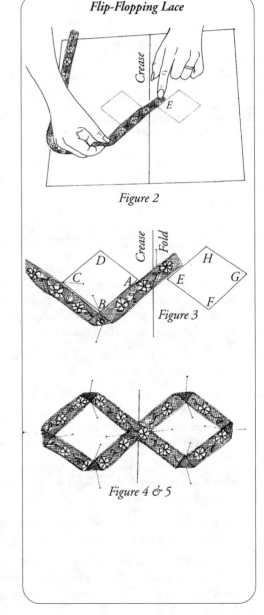

Flip-Flopping Lace

Figure 2

Figure 3

Figure 4 & 5

9. Spray starch and press the bow, that is shaped with the pins still in the board, with its bow tie in place (**fig. 6**). Remove pins from the board and pin the bow flat to the skirt or other garment. You are now ready to attach the shaped bow to the garment.

10. This illustration gives you ideas for making a bow two ways. First, the "A" side of the bow has just the garment fabric peeking through the center of the bow. Second, the "B" side of the bow illustrates what the bow will look like if you put a pintucked strip in the center. Both are beautiful (**fig. 7**).

11. If you prefer the bow to look like side (A), which has the fabric of the garment showing through the middle of the bow, follow these steps for completing the bow. Zigzag around the total outside of the bow. Then, zigzag around the inside portions of both sides of the bow. Finally, zigzag around the finished bow "tie" portion (**fig. 8**). The bows will be attached to the dress.

12. If you prefer the bow to look like side (B), which will have pintucks (or anything else you choose) inside, follow the directions in this section. (These directions are when you have bows on areas other than the bottom of a skirt or sleeve or collar. If you have bows at the bottom of anything, then you have to follow the skirt directions given in the diamond skirt section.)

13. Zigzag the outside only of the bows all the way around. Notice that your bow "tie" will be partially stitched since part of it is on the outside edges.

14. I suggest pintucking a larger piece of fabric and cutting small sections which are somewhat larger than the insides of the bows (**fig. 9**).

15. Cut away fabric from behind both center sections of the bow. I lovingly tell my students that now they can place their whole fists inside the holes in the centers of this bow.

16. Place the pintucked section behind the center of the lace bows. Zigzag around the inside of the bows, which will now attach the pintucked section. From the back, trim away the excess pintucked section. You now have pintucks in the center of each side of the bow (**fig. 10**).

17. Go back and stitch the sides of the bow "tie" down. After you have zigzagged all the way around your bow "tie," you can trim away excess laces which crossed underneath the tie. This gives the bow tie a little neater look. ❁

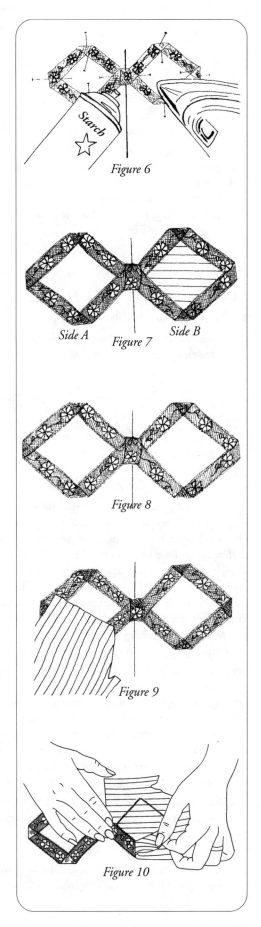

Figure 6

Side A   Figure 7   Side B

Figure 8

Figure 9

Figure 10

Tied Lace Bows

This method of bow shaping I saw for the first time years ago in Australia. It is beautiful and each bow will be a little different which makes it a very interesting variation of the flip-flopped bow. Your options on shaping the bow part of this cute bow are as follows:

1. You can flip-flop the bow
2. You can curve the bow and pull a string to make it round
3. You can flip-flop one side and curve the other side. Bows can be made of lace insertion, lace edging, or lace beading. If you make your tied lace bow of lace edging, be sure to put the scalloped side of the lace edging for the outside of the bow and leave the string to pull on the inside.

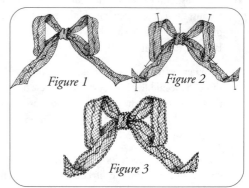

Figure 1   Figure 2

Figure 3

Materials Needed

❀ 1 yard to 1¹/₄ yards lace insertion, edging or beading for one bow

Directions

1. Tie the lace into a bow, leaving equal streamers on either side of the bow.

2. Using a lace board, shape the bow onto the garment, using either the flip-flopped method or the pulled thread curved method.

3. Shape the streamers of the bow using either the flip-flopped method or the pulled thread method.

4. Shape the ends of the streamer into an angle.

5. Zigzag or machine entredeux stitch the shaped bow and streamers to the garment. ❀

Hearts-Fold Back Miter Method

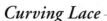

Curving Lace

Since many heirloom sewers are also incurable romantics, it's no wonder hearts are a popular lace shape. Hearts are the ultimate design for a wedding dress, wedding attendants' clothing, or on a ring bearer's pillow. As with the other lace shaping discussed in this chapter, begin with a template when making hearts. When using our heart template, we like to shape our laces inside the heart design. Of course, shaping along the outside of the heart design is permitted also, so do whatever is easiest for you.

With the writing of the *Antique Clothing* book, I thought I had really figured out the easy way to make lace hearts. After four years of teaching heart making, I have totally changed my method of making hearts. This new method is so very easy that I just couldn't wait to tell you about it. After shaping your hearts, you don't even have to remove them from the skirt to finish the heart. What a relief and an improvement! Enjoy the new method of making hearts with the new fold back miters. It is so easy and you are going to have so much fun making hearts.

1. Draw a template in the shape of a heart. Make this as large or as small as you want. If you want equal hearts around the bottom of a skirt, fold the skirt into equal sections, and design the heart template to fit into one section of the skirt when using your chosen width of lace insertion.

2. Draw on your hearts all the way around the skirt if you are using several hearts. As always, when shaping lace, draw the hearts onto the fabric where you will be stitching the laces.

3. Draw a 2" bisecting line at the top into the center and at the bottom of the heart into the center (**fig. 1**).

NOTE: I would like to refresh your memory on lace shaping along the bottom of a skirt at this time. You make your hearts (or whatever else you wish to make) above the skirt while the skirt still has a straight bottom. Later after stitching your hearts (or whatever else) to the skirt, you cut away to make the shaped skirt bottom.

4. Lay the fabric with the hearts drawn on top, on top of the fabric board. As always, pin the lace shaping through the lace, the fabric and into the fabric board.

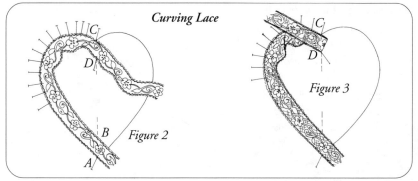

Curving Lace

Figure 2

Figure 3

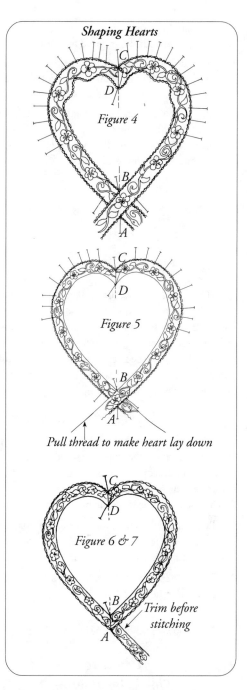

Shaping Hearts

Figure 4

Figure 5

Pull thread to make heart lay down

Figure 6 & 7

Trim before stitching

5. Cut one piece of lace which will be large enough to go all the way around one heart with about 4" extra. Before you begin shaping the lace, leave about 2" of lace on the outside of the bottom line.

6. Place a pin at **point A**. Beginning at the bottom of the heart, pin the lace on the inside of the heart template. The pins will actually be on the outside of the lace insertion; however, you are shaping your laces on the inside of your drawn heart template.

7. Work around the heart to **point C**, placing pins at $^1/_2$" intervals. Notice that the outside will be pinned rather tightly and the inside will be curvy. **Note:** One of our math teacher students told me years ago, while I was teaching this lace shaping, a very important fact. She said, "Martha did you know that a curved line is just a bunch of straight lines placed in a funny way?" She said this as I was trying to explain that it was pretty easy to get the straight lace pinned into a curve. Since I remembered as little about my math classes as possible, I am sure that I didn't know this fact. It makes it a lot easier to explain taking that straight lace and making a curve out of it to know that fact.

8. After finishing pinning around to the center of the heart, place another pin at **point D** (**fig. 2**).

9. Lay the lace back on itself, curving it into the curve that you just pinned (**fig. 3**). Remove the pin from **point C** and repin it, this time pinning through both layers of lace.

10. Wrap the lace to the other side and begin pinning around the other side of the heart. Where you took the lace back on itself and repinned, there will be a miter which appears just like magic. This is the new fold back miter which is just as wonderful on hearts as it is on diamonds and scalloped skirts.

11. Pin the second side of the lace just like you pinned the first one. At the bottom of the heart, lay the laces one over the other and put a pin at **point B** (**fig. 4**).

12. It is now time to pull the threads to make the curvy insides of the heart lay flat and become heart shaped. You can pull threads either from the bottom of the heart or threads from the center of each side of the heart. I prefer to pull the threads from the bottom of the heart. Pull the threads and watch the heart lay down flat and pretty. (**fig. 5**). After teaching literally hundreds of students to make hearts, I think it is better to pull the thread from the bottom of the heart. You don't need to help the fullness lay down; simply pull the thread. On other lace shaped curves such as a scalloped skirt, loops, or ovals, you have to pull from the inside curve.

13. Spray starch and press the curves into place.

14. To make your magic miter at the bottom of the heart, remove the pin from **point A**, fold back the lace so it lays on the other piece of lace, and repin **point A**. You now have a folded back miter which completes the easy mitering on the heart (**fig. 6**). You are now ready to pin the hearts flat onto the garment and remove the shaping from the fabric board.

15. You can trim these bottom "tails" of lace away before you attach the heart to the garment or after you attach the heart to the garment. It probably looks better to trim them before you stitch (**fig. 7**).

16. You can attach the hearts just to the fabric or you can choose to put something else such as pintucks inside the hearts. If you have hearts which touch going all the way around a skirt, then follow the directions for zigzagging which are in the diamond section.

17. If you have one heart on a collar or bodice of a dress, then zigzag the outside first. If you choose to put something on the inside of each heart, cut away the fabric from behind the shape after zigzagging it to the garment. Then, put whatever you want to insert in the heart behind the heart shape and zigzag around the center or inside of

the heart. Refer to the directions on inserting pintucks or something else in the center of a lace shape in the flip-flopped bow section.

18. You can certainly use the entredeux/wing needle stitching for a beautiful look for attaching the hearts. Follow the directions for machine entredeux on the lace shaped skirt found in the diamond section of this lace shaping chapter.

19. After you cut away the fabric from behind the hearts, go back and zigzag over each mitered point (**fig. 8**). You then have the choice of either leaving the folded over section or of cutting it away. Personally, I usually leave the section because of the strength it adds to the miters. The choice is yours. ✺

Figure 8

Scalloped Skirt

I have always loved scalloped skirts. The first one that I ever saw intimidated me so much that I didn't even try to make one for several years after that. The methods which I am presenting to you in this section are so easy that I think you won't be afraid to try making one of my favorite garments. Scalloping lace can be a very simple way to finish the bottom of a smocked dress or can be a very elaborate way to put row after row of lace scallops with curved pintucks in between those scallops. Plain or very elaborate - this is one of my favorite things in French sewing by machine. Enjoy!

Preparing The Skirt For Lace Scallops

Before I give you the steps below, which is one great way to prepare scallops on a skirt, let me share with you that you can also follow the instructions found under the beginning lace techniques for scallops as well as diamonds, hearts, teardrops or circles. These instructions are so that you can use any size scallop that you want to for any width skirt. How do you do that? Stitch or serge up one side seam of your whole skirt before placing the scallops.

1. Pull a thread and cut or tear your skirt. I usually put 88 inches in my skirt, two 44-inch widths - one for the front and one for the back. Make the skirt length the proper one for your garment. Sew one side seam.

2. Trace one scallop on each side of the side seam. Continue tracing until you are almost at the edge of the fabric. Leave a seam allowance beyond the last scallops and trim away the excess (**fig. 1**).

3. Now you are ready to shape the lace along the template lines.

Pinning The Lace Insertion To The Skirt Portion On The Fabric Board

1. Cut enough lace insertion to go around all of the scallops on the skirt. Allow at least 16 inches more than you measured. You can later use the excess lace insertion in another area of the dress. If you do not have a piece of insertion this long, remember to piece your laces so that the pieced section will go into the miter at the top of the scallop.

2. Pin the lace insertion to the skirt (one scallop at a time only) by poking pins all the way into the fabric board, through the bottom lace heading and the fabric of the skirt. Notice on (**figure 2**) that the bottom of the lace is straight with the pins poked into the board. The top of the lace is rather "curvy" because it hasn't been shaped to lie flat yet.

3. As you take the lace into the top of the first scallop, carefully place a pin into the lace and the board at **points C and D**. Pinning the D point is very important. That is why you drew the line bisecting the top of each scallop (**fig. 2**). Pin the B point at exactly the place where the flat lace crosses the line you drew to bisect the scallop.

Preparing The Skirt For Lace Scallops

Seam

Figure 1

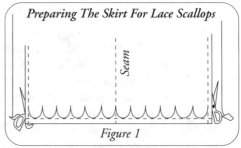

Pinning The Lace Insertion

D *D*

C *C*

Figure 2

D

C

Figure 3

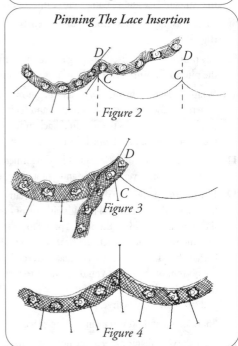

Figure 4

4. Fold back the whole piece of lace onto the other side (**fig. 3**). Remove the pin at C and repin it to go through both layers of lace. Leave the pin at point D just as it is.

5. Then fold over the lace to place the next section of the lace to travel into the next part of the scallop (**fig.4**).

NOTE: If a little bit of that folded point is exposed after you place the lace into the next scallop, just push it underneath the miter until the miter looks perfect (**fig. 5**). I lovingly call this "mushing" the miter into place.

6. To shape the excess fullness of the top of the scallop, simply pull a gathering thread at the center point of each scallop until the lace becomes flat and pretty (**fig. 6**).

7. Place a pin in the lace loop you just pulled until you spray starch and press the scallop flat. Remember, it is easier to pull the very top thread of the lace, the one which makes a prominent scallop on the top of the lace. If you break that thread, go in and pull another one. Many laces have as many as 4 or 5 total threads which you can pull. Don't worry about that little pulled thread; when you zigzag the lace to the skirt or entredeux stitch it to the skirt, simply trim away that little pulled thread. The heaviness of the zigzag or the entredeux stitch will secure the lace to the skirt.

8. Spray starch and press each scallop and miter after you finish shaping them.

9. After finishing with the section of scallops you have room for on that one board, pin the laces flat to the skirt and begin another section of your skirt (**fig 7**). You have the choice here of either zigzagging each section of the skirt as you complete it, or waiting until you finish the whole skirt.

10. If you choose to use a decorative stitch on your sewing machine (entredeux stitch with a wing needle) you will need to stitch with some sort of stabilizer underneath the skirt. Stitch 'n Tear is an excellent one. Some use tissue paper, others prefer wax paper or adding machine paper. Actually, the paper you buy at a medical supply store that doctors use for covering their examining tables is great also. As long as you are stitching using a wing needle and heavy decorative stitching, you really need a stabilizer.

11. If you have an entredeux stitch on your sewing machine, you can stitch entredeux at both the top and bottom of this scalloped skirt (**fig. 8**). There are two methods of doing this.

Method Number One

1. After you finish your entredeux/wing needle stitching on both the top and the bottom of the scalloped skirt, trim away the fabric from behind the lace scallop.

2. Carefully trim the fabric from the bottom of the skirt also, leaving just a "hair" of seam allowance (**fig. 9**).

3. You are now ready to zigzag over the folded in miters (**fig. 10**). Use a regular needle for this zigzag.

4. Now zigzag the gathered laces to the bottom of this machine created entredeux.

Method Number Two

1. Machine entredeux the top only of the scallop (**fig. 11a**). Don't cut anything away.

2. Butt your gathered lace edging, a few inches at a time, to the shaped bottom of the lace scallop. Machine entredeux stitch in between the flat scalloped lace and the gathered edging lace, thus attaching both laces at the same time you are stitching in the machine entredeux (**fig. 11b**). Be sure you put more fullness at the points of the scallop.

3. After the gathered lace edging is completely stitched to the bottom of the skirt with your machine entredeux, cut away the bottom of the skirt fabric as closely to the stitching as possible (**fig. 12**).

4. Zigzag over your folded in miters (**fig. 12a**).

5. If you are going to attach the lace to the fabric with just a plain zigzag stitch, you might try (Width=$1^1/2$ to 2, Length=1 to $1^1/2$). You want the zigzag to be wide enough to completely go over the heading of the laces and short enough to be strong. If you are zigzagging the laces to the skirt, zigzag the **top only** of the lace scallops (see **fig. 13**).

6. After you zigzag the top only of this skirt, carefully trim away the bottom portion of the fabric skirt, trimming all the way up to the stitches (**fig. 13**).

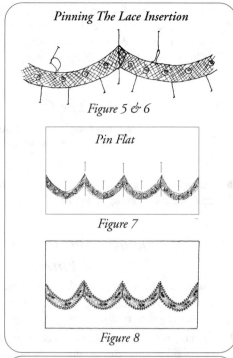

Pinning The Lace Insertion

Figure 5 & 6

Pin Flat

Figure 7

Figure 8

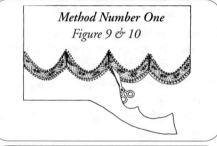

Method Number One
Figure 9 & 10

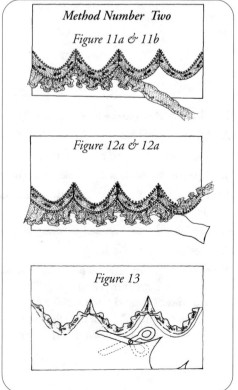

Method Number Two

Figure 11a & 11b

Figure 12a & 12a

Figure 13

7. Now you have a scalloped skirt. Later you might want to add entredeux to the bottom of the scalloped skirt. It is perfectly alright just to add gathered laces to this lace scallop without either entredeux or machine stitched entredeux. Just treat the bottom of this lace scallop as a finished edge; gather your lace edging and zigzag to the bottom of the lace (**see fig. 14**).

Finishing The Center Of The Miter
After Attaching It To The Skirt and Trimming Away
The Fabric From Behind the Scallops

I always zigzag down the center of this folded miter. You can leave the folded lace portion in the miter to make the miter stronger or you can trim away the folded portion after you have zigzagged over the miter center (**fig. 14**).

Sewing Hand-Gathered French Lace
To Entredeux Edge

1. Gather lace by hand by pulling the thread in the heading of the lace. I use the scalloped outside thread of the heading first since I think it gathers better than the inside threads. Distribute gathers evenly.

2. Trim the side of the entredeux to which the gathered lace is to be attached. Side by side, right sides up, zigzag the gathered lace to the trimmed entredeux (Width=$1^1/_2$; Length=2) (**fig. 15**).

3. Using a wooden shish kabob stick, push the gathers evenly into the sewing machine as you zigzag. You can also use a pick or long pin of some sort to push the gathers evenly into the sewing machine.

Hint: To help distribute the gathers evenly fold the entredeux in half and half again. Mark these points with a fabric marker. Before the lace is gathered, fold it in half and half again. Mark the folds with a fabric marker. Now gather the lace and match the marks on the entredeux and the marks on the lace (**fig. 16**). ✽

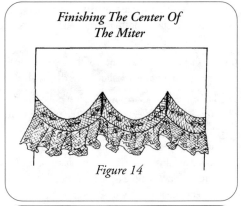

Finishing The Center Of The Miter

Figure 14

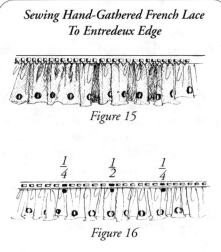

Sewing Hand-Gathered French Lace To Entredeux Edge

Figure 15

Figure 16

French Seam

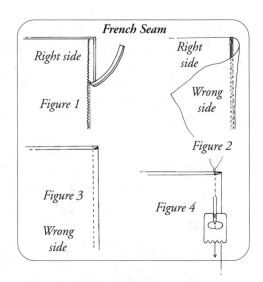

1. Place the fabric pieces with wrong sides together.

2. Stitch a row of tiny zigzag stitches (L 1.0, W 1.0) $^3/_{16}$" outside the seam line (**see fig. 1**).

3. Press the seam flat and trim away the seam allowance outside the zigzags (**fig. 1**).

4. Open out the fabric and press the seam to one side.

5. Fold the fabric along the seam line with right sides together, encasing the zigzag stitching (**fig. 2**).

6. Stitch a $^3/_{16}$" seam, enclosing the zigzag stitching (**fig. 3**).

7. Press the seam to one side.

Note: A serged, rolled edge may be used for the first seam, when the fabric pieces are wrong sides together. No trimming will be needed, as the serger cuts off the excess seam allowance. If a pintuck foot is available, use it to stitch the second seam for either the zigzag or serger method. Place the tiny folded seam into a groove of the foot so that the needle will stitch right along beside the little roll of fabric (**fig. 4**). ✽

French Seam

Right side *Right side*

Figure 1 *Wrong side*

Figure 2

Figure 3 *Figure 4*

Wrong side

Extra-Stable Lace Finishing

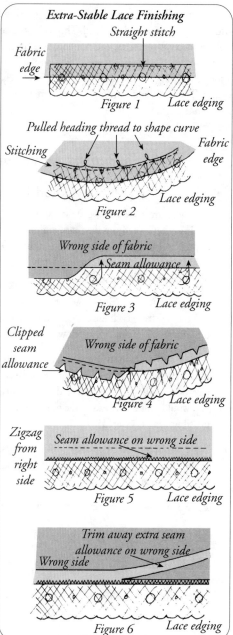

Extra-Stable Lace Finish for Fabric Edges

1. If the lace is being attached to a straight edge of fabric, pin the heading of the lace to the right side, ¹⁄₄" or more from the cut edge, with the right side of the lace facing up and the outside edge of the lace extending over the edge of the fabric. Using a short straight stitch, stitch the heading to the fabric (**fig. 1**).

2. If the lace is being attached to a curved edge, shape the lace around the curve as you would for lace shaping; refer to "Lace Shaping" found on page 40. Pull up the threads in the lace heading if necessary. Continue pinning and stitching the lace as directed in Step 1 above (**fig. 2**).

3. Press the seam allowance away from the lace, toward the wrong side of the fabric (**fig. 3**). If the edge is curved or pointed, you may need to clip the seam allowance in order to press flat (**fig. 4**).

4. On the right side, use a short, narrow zigzag to stitch over the lace heading, catching the fold of the pressed seam allowance (**fig. 5**).

5. On the wrong side, trim the seam allowance close to the zigzag (**fig. 6**).

Note: Extra-Stable Lace Finish for Fabric Edges can be used for lace shaping. ✸

Extra-Stable Lace Finish for Fabric Edges

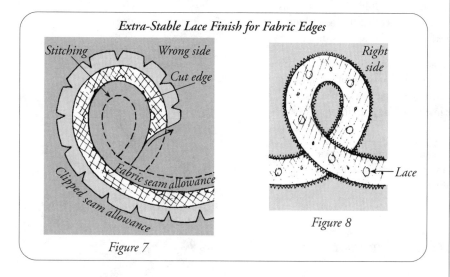

Figure 7

Figure 8

Making Baby Piping

If self-made piping will be used, measure all of the places it will be applied and use these instructions for making it:

Cut a bias strip 1¹⁄₄" wide by the length needed. Bias may be pieced so that the piping will be made in one long strip. Place tiny cording along the center of the strip on the wrong side and fold the fabric over the cording, meeting the long edges of the fabric. Use a zipper foot to stitch close to the cording (**fig. a**). ✸

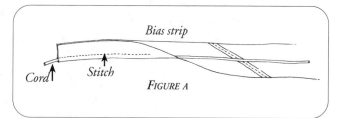

FIGURE A

Shaped Puffing

Narrow puffing strips can be shaped in many of the same ways in which wide lace insertion can be shaped. This technique for puffing should be used only for decorative effects, and not on sleeve cuffs, for yoke-to-skirt attachments, or any place where there is stress on the fabric, because it is not as strong as puffing made with entredeux. It is a lovely treatment for skirts or collars. The loops and teardrops shown here have a little Swiss embroidered motif in the center; however, you could use lace insertion or a lace rosette in the center.

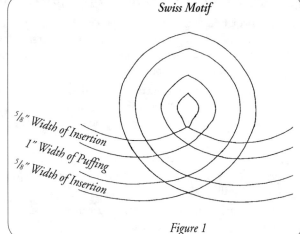

Swiss Motif

⅝" Width of Insertion
1" Width of Puffing
⅝" Width of Insertion

Figure 1

Puffing Directions

Method I

1. On paper, trace around the Swiss motif. Draw another line the width of the insertion away from the motif outline. Draw another line 1" (or desired width of puffing) beside second line. Draw another line the width of insertion outside the third line. Draw lines at the bottom to continue into smooth scallops (**fig. 1**).

2. Cut lots of puffing strips ³/₄" wider than your finished puffing. Run gathering threads ¹/₈" and ¹/₂" from each long edge. Use cotton covered polyester thread, loosened top tension, stitch length 2.5, stitch with bobbin thread on right side of strips (**fig. 2**).

3. Gather puffing strip to approximately 2:1 fullness and distribute gathers evenly. Place puffing strip over fabric (over fabric board), and pin in place as you would shaped insertion. Pull up gathering threads on inner curves to make puffing lay flat, just as you would pull the thread in the heading of lace insertion. Use your fingernail to distribute gathers (**fig. 3**).

4. Baste or pin puffing in place close to raw edges. Shape insertion along drawn lines. Remove pins from fabric board. Zigzag in place except for very center of loop (**fig 4**). Trim all layers from behind lace and puffing.

5. Place Swiss motif in center of loop and zigzag to lace.

Narrow Puffing With A Gathering Foot

Method II

You can use the gathering foot on your sewing machine to make this narrow puffing around the curves. Cut strip 1" wide than desired finished puffing. It really does work!

1. Using a gathering foot ¹/₂" from the edge. Trim the seam allowance to ¹/₄". Using a gathering foot run a row of gathers down both sides of the strip.

2. Pin as shown in (**fig. 3**).

3. With your fingers, "mush" the inside gathers into place.

4. Follow directions as in 4 and 5 above. ✹

Teardrop Or
Candlelight Puffing

Loop Puffing

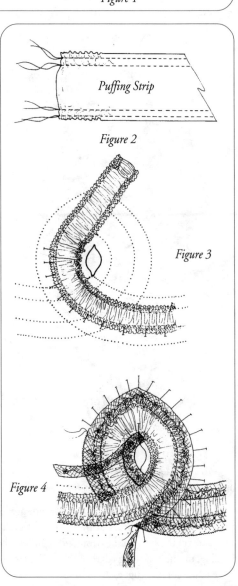

Puffing Strip

Figure 2

Figure 3

Figure 4

Cutwork

Cutwork is a type of embroidery in which an area of fabric is cut away and the edges are bound with a satin stitch. Using the sewing machine to first reinforce an area to be cut away, trimming the fabric and then satin stitching the edge makes it quick and easy. Cutwork can be used on collars, cuffs, blouse fronts and skirt hems.

General Supplies

- ✳ Darning foot, open darning foot or darning spring
- ✳ Machine embroidery hoop (wooden or spring)
- ✳ Needles (#70 to #90)
- ✳ Light weight or machine embroidery thread
- ✳ Stabilizer (water soluble, tear away, or liquid)

- ✳ Water soluble pen or pencil
- ✳ Small, sharp pointed scissors
- ✳ Extra fine permanent marker
- ✳ White water soluble pen
- ✳ Bobbin case (optional)
- ✳ Open toe appliqué foot
- ✳ Interfacing
- ✳ Appliqué Scissors

Stabilizers

Water soluable stabilizer (WSS) is preferred since it can be washed away without putting stress on the stitches or bars when it is removed. It will not leave any residue or stiffness when removed completely. Use 2 to 4 layers, depending on body of base fabric and the heaviness and width of the stitches.

Fabric Used for Cutwork

The most often used fabric for cutwork is linen or linen-like fabrics. The fabric should not be too loosely woven and should have enough body to support the stitches. More than one layer of fabric can be used to add body. The fabric can be interfaced with a lightweight fusible interfacing prior to any stitching. If the fabric for a collar is interfaced, back it with another layer of fabric. The fabric should be pretreated before any marking or stitching is done due to shrinkage and to remove finish from the factory.

General Cutwork Directions

Fabric Preparation

1. To determine the size of fabric for the cutwork, consider the position of the cutwork. The fabric should extend beyond the cutwork design in all directions so that it may be placed in the hoop. For example, when doing cutwork on a pocket edge, even though the pocket pattern itself is small, you must start with a piece of fabric large enough to fit in a hoop (**fig. 1**). Another example would be when placing cutwork on the edge of a sleeve, the fabric must be large enough to contain the whole cutwork design plus enough fabric on the edges to be held in the hoop (**fig. 2**).

2. Press and starch the pretreated fabric to remove all of the wrinkles and give the fabric some body. Several applications of starch can be used.

3. Interface the fabric if needed.

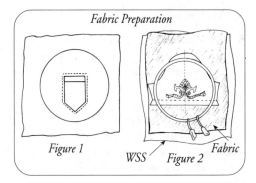

Fabric Preparation

Figure 1   WSS   *Figure 2*   Fabric

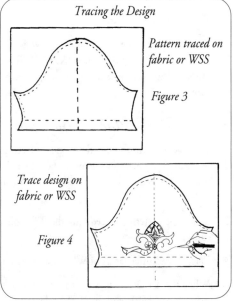

Tracing the Design

Pattern traced on fabric or WSS

Figure 3

Trace design on fabric or WSS

Figure 4

Tracing the Design

1. Trace the pattern piece and design onto the fabric.

a. See-through fabric: Place the pattern under the fabric. Trace the pattern onto the fabric using a water or air soluable pen (**fig. 3**). Use of a light box, if available, is helpful. Follow manufacturers' instructions for the marking pen or pencil. Sometimes heat from an iron may set these marks, so always test first!

b. Opaque fabric (cannot see through): When using a dark colored or opaque fabric the design must be traced onto a layer of WSS. The WSS is then placed on top of the fabric in the desired position (**fig. 4**). Use the Pigma pen when tracing a design to be placed on a light colored opaque fabric. Use the white washable marker to trace the design to be placed on top of a dark fabric.

2. Mark the cutting and seam lines.

3. Mark the center front or any other important marking lines.

4. DO NOT CUT OUT AT THIS TIME (**fig. 5**).

5. Mark all areas to be cut out with an "X" (**fig. 6**).

6. Richelieu bar placement can also be marked with a line extending beyond the area to be cut away (**fig. 7**). Richelieu bars connect both sides of an open area, helping to stabilize the area. Bars are not necessary for small cut away areas.

a. Straight Richeleiu Bars:

These bars should be no longer than about ¹/₂ inch long. When the bar is too long, it will not stabilize the area adequately. These bars can be straight across, connecting one side of the opening to the opposite side (**fig. 8**) For an open area that has one side larger than another, as a half circle, the bars can be placed at angles to form an open "V" or "V's" (**fig. 9**). Use as many bars as necessary to stabilize the open area (**fig. 10**).

b. Divided Richelieu Bar:

A wider width open area may be too wide for a straight bar. In this case, a DIVIDED bar will be formed to look like a "Y" (**fig. 11**). For a large open area, the space must be stabilized with bars of any shape connected to each other AND the sides of the open area (**fig. 12**).

Placing the Fabric in a Hoop

1. For machine embroidery, the fabric is placed in the hoop opposite from hand embroidery. The right side of the fabric will be facing up, the wrong side is down toward the bed of the machine (**fig. 13**). Stabilizer should be added under the two layers.

2. When the pattern is traced onto the WSS, pin or baste the WSS in position on top of the fabric.

3. Place one to three layers of WSS to wrong side of the fabric.

4. When the design size is larger than the hoop, baste all layers together so that the pattern, the fabric and the WSS under the fabric will not shift when changing the hoop position (**fig. 14**).

Preparing the Sewing Machine for Cutwork

Thread and Tension

Thread machine with matching machine embroidery thread in top and bobbin. The tension is balanced at this time.

Cutwork with an Appliqué Foot

1. Place open toe appliqué foot on machine.

2. With a straight stitch, length of 1 to 1.5 mm, stitch around all areas to be cut away. Stitching over ALL of the lines in the design (not just areas to be cut away) will add a padding under the final satin stitch (**fig. 15**). This straight stitch will prevent stretching when the fabric is cut away from the design.

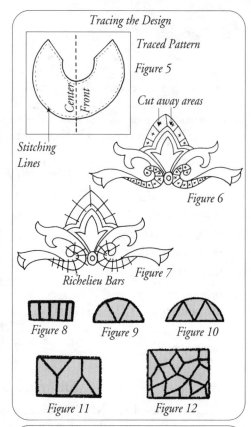

Tracing the Design

Traced Pattern

Figure 5

Center Front

Stitching Lines

Cut away areas

Figure 6

Richelieu Bars

Figure 7

Figure 8   Figure 9   Figure 10

Figure 11   Figure 12

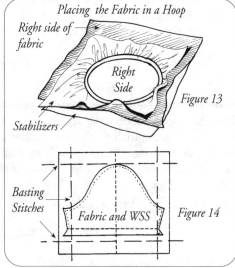

Placing the Fabric in a Hoop

Right side of fabric

Right Side

Figure 13

Stabilizers

Basting Stitches

Fabric and WSS

Figure 14

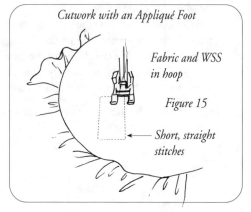

Cutwork with an Appliqué Foot

Fabric and WSS in hoop

Figure 15

Short, straight stitches

3. Stitch over the straight stitch with a short narrow zig zag, width of 0.5 to 1 mm and length of 1 mm (**fig. 16**). This is not a satin stitch. Stitch all of the design lines that are in the hoop. You can move the hoop to complete all of the design lines before cutting any area away. The zigzag stitch will help prevent the fabric from pulling away from the stitches when the areas are cut away.

4. With the fabric still in the hoop, trim the fabric close to the stitching from the appropriate areas leaving the lower layer(s) of WSS in place (**fig. 17**. The lower, uncut layers of WSS will prevent distortion of the cut away areas. If the design were on the top layer of WSS, this will be cut away also. Use sharp, small pointed scissors to cut away, being careful not to cut the stitches. Appliqué scissors are very useful.

5. LOOK AT THE DESIGN. The Richelieu bars and the satin stitches to cover the bars and raw edges are worked background to foreground. Place design back under the needle at the appropriate starting point.

6. Set up the sewing machine for a satin stitch: Loosen top thread tension so that the bobbin thread will pull the top thread to the back for a smoother stitch on the right side. Set stitch length at satin stitch. The stitch width will be adjusted during the stitching.

7. Richelieu bars are completed before the final satin stitching is done.

Straight Richelieu Bars

a. Pull up bobbin thread near first bar, place both upper and lower threads under and behind the foot (**fig. 18**). Take three to six short straight stitches (satin stitch length) to TIE-ON (this is done each time you start a new area), ending at first bar placement (**fig. 19**). Cut thread ends close to the first stitch.

b. Lift foot and move fabric across the opening so that needle will pierce opposite side beyond the previous zigzag stitch (**fig. 20**). Lower foot and take one stitch. This is a "WALK" stitch over the opening. You have not actually "stitched" through the opening, but just moved the thread over it. You can see two separate threads, the top and the bobbin thread. Repeat at least two more times so that there will be three walked stitches over the opening (6 threads) (**fig. 21**). These walked stitches will form the base for the bars. More or fewer walk stitches can be taken to make a thicker or narrower finished bar.

c. Change the stitch width to cover the walked stitches (1 to 2 mm), usually a little narrower than the final satin stitching will be. This width will be determined by the number of walked stitches. Satin stitch over the walked stitches only within the opening (**fig. 22**) being certain all walk threads are caught in the satin stitch and covered completely.

d. Straight stitch on the fabric to the next bar within the same opening. Repeat as above. Finish all bars within this area (**fig. 23**).

You can finish all of the walk stitches within an area before satin stitching or finish each bar individually.

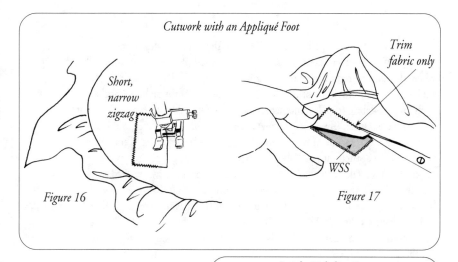

Cutwork with an Appliqué Foot

Short, narrow zigzag

Figure 16

Trim fabric only

WSS

Figure 17

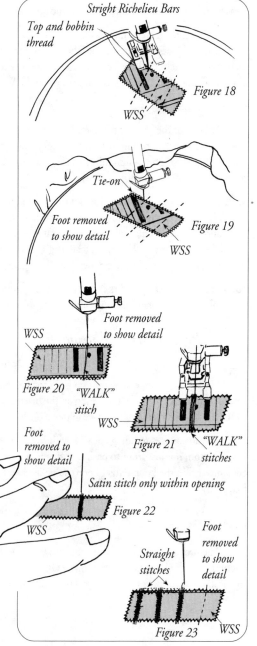

Stright Richelieu Bars

Top and bobbin thread

WSS

Figure 18

Tie-on

Foot removed to show detail

WSS

Figure 19

WSS

Foot removed to show detail

Figure 20

"WALK" stitch

WSS

"WALK" stitches

Figure 21

Foot removed to show detail

Satin stitch only within opening

WSS

Figure 22

Straight stitches

Foot removed to show detail

WSS

Figure 23

Divided Richelieu Bars

For a bar that is shaped like a "Y", begin at the upper left leg of the "Y". After tying on, move (WALK) from the tie-on stitch to the desired place on WSS within the opening (where the left and right legs of the "Y" join). Take a stitch IN the WSS (**fig. 24**). This will be the first SEGMENT of the bar. Walk to the top of the right leg of the "Y". Take a stitch into the fabric (**fig. 25**)(another segment). Walk back to the end of the first segment, take a stitch (**fig. 26**). You now have TWO walked stitches in this segment. Walk to the opposite side of the opening, creating the last segment of the "Y" bar (**fig. 27**). Take a stitch into the fabric just beyond the zigzag stitching. Walk to intersection in the WSS, take a stitch. Now two of the segments have two walked stitches (four threads). At this point, you can walk in any direction to increase the walk stitches in the segments and you can satin stitch one segment (if it has six threads) before ALL of the segments have six threads. You must **finish** the satin stitching at the fabric edge and not in the WSS (**fig. 28**). Sometimes it will be necessary to add an additional walked stitch so that the satin stitching will finish at the fabric edge and not in the WSS. The cut away area should have enough bars to support the opening.

For large open areas, make a network of walked stitches, connecting them to each other within the opening and to the fabric at the edges of the opening (**fig. 29**). All of these walked stitches MUST be connected to another segment or to the fabric at the edge of the opening. If they are not connected, when the WSS is rinsed away it will fall apart.

8. Satin stitch

After all of the bars are completed, adjust the stitch width so that it will be wide enough to cover the previous stitching (straight and zigzag stitch) AND the raw edges of the opening. The most commonly used is a stitch width of 2 mm or less. Satin stitch to cover the raw edges (**fig. 30**).

9. After all the necessary stitching is done and before moving to another area you must TIE-OFF the threads. Change stitch width to zero (satin stitch length), reposition fabric so that needle will go back into same hole it just came out of, and take three to six stitches next to the satin stitches (**fig. 31**). These tie off stitches should be done on the fabric and not in the cut away opening.

10. Remember to always work background to foreground. This may mean to satin stitch only a portion of an opening before going to another area (**fig. 32**).

Free Motion Cutwork using a Darning Foot or Darning Spring

Machine cutwork can be done in free motion, that is, with the feed dogs lowered or covered and the darning foot or spring on the machine. When doing free motion work, **YOU** are the stitch length. You have to move the hoop to create a stitch length.

The advantages to doing cutwork with free motion are the hoop can be moved in any direction, not just front to back as with a foot on and more of the design can be encompassed in the hoop (larger hoop can be used and position will not need to change as frequently).

Free motion does require more practice and control than does cutwork with the foot.

The procedure of free motion cutwork is the same as with the appliqué foot. Everything is done the same except that **YOU** move the hoop to create the stitch length of the straight stitch, the open zigzag and the satin stitch zigzag.

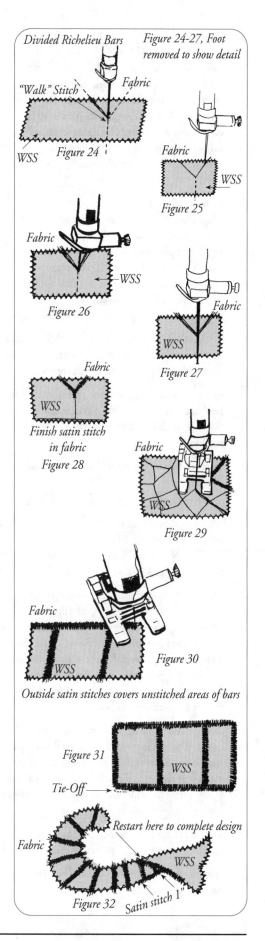

Divided Richelieu Bars   Figure 24-27, Foot removed to show detail

"Walk" Stitch   Fabric

WSS   Figure 24

Fabric   WSS

Figure 25

Fabric   WSS

Figure 26

WSS   Fabric

Figure 27

Fabric

WSS   Finish satin stitch in fabric   Figure 28

Fabric   WSS   Figure 29

Fabric   WSS   Figure 30

Outside satin stitches covers unstitched areas of bars

Figure 31   WSS   Tie-Off

Fabric   Restart here to complete design   WSS   Figure 32   Satin stitch 1"

Optional Cutwork Techniques

The following techniques can be done with the applique foot or free motion stitching.

Small Areas

Small areas can be cut away and then satin stitched without bars.

1. For a small area such as a tear drop, first straight stitch and then open zigzag.

2. Slit the fabric and the WSS in the opening down the middle with a "Y" at each end (**fig. 33**).

3. Satin stitch the opening, drawing in and encasing the raw edges as you stitch (**fig. 34**).

Larger Areas

Larger areas without bars can be treated in a similar manner.

1. First straight stitch and then open zigzag.

2. Slit the fabric and the WSS in the opening down the middle with a "Y" at each end (**fig. 35**).

3. Fold fabric and WSS to wrong side and glue stick to hold in place (**fig. 36**).

4. Satin stitch as described to encase the previous stitching and the folded edge.

5. Trim any excess fabric and WSS from the wrong side close to the satin stitch (**fig. 37**).

Larger Area with Bars

Larger areas with bars can be treated in a similar manner.

1. Straight stitch, open zigzag, and slit the fabric and the WSS as described above.

2. Fold fabric and WSS to wrong side and glue stick to hold in place (**fig. 38**).

3. Form the Richelieu bars as described previously.

4. Satin stitch to encase the previous stitching and the folded edge.

5. Trim any excess fabric and WSS from the wrong side close to the satin stitch.

Corded Edge Cutwork

A cord can be encased in the finishing satin stitch if desired. This will add strength to the open area.

1. Lay the cord next to the raw edge of the opening (**fig. 39**).

2. Encase the cord when doing the satin stitch.

Netting or Sheer Fabric for Support

A layer of netting or other sheer fabric can be placed behind the main fabric so that when an area is cut away, the netting or sheer fabric will support the opening. This will also eliminate the need for Richelieu bars in large cut away areas.

1. The netting or sheer fabric is placed to the wrong side of the base fabric before any stitching is done.

2. To facilitate cutting the base fabric away without cutting the netting or sheer fabric, place an extra layer of WSS **BETWEEN** the base fabric and the netting.

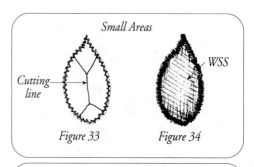

Small Areas

Figure 33   *Figure 34*

WSS

Cutting line

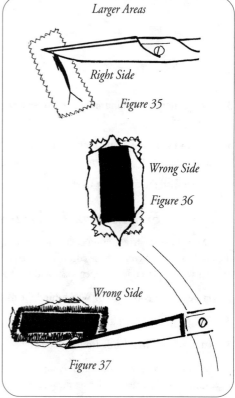

Larger Areas

Right Side

Figure 35

Wrong Side

Figure 36

Wrong Side

Figure 37

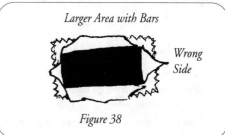

Larger Area with Bars

Wrong Side

Figure 38

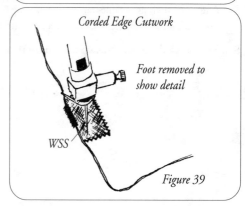

Corded Edge Cutwork

Foot removed to show detail

WSS

Figure 39

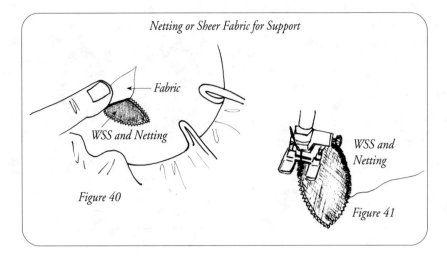

Figure 40

WSS and Netting

Figure 41

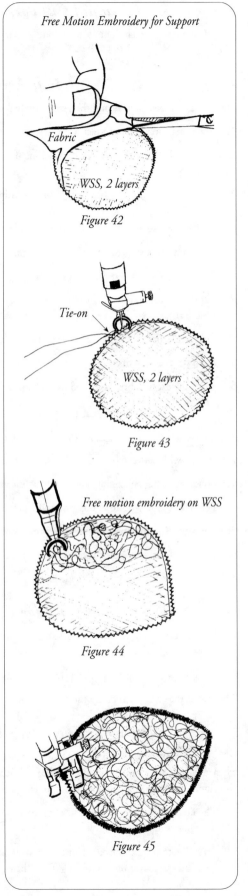

3. As the straight stitching and narrow open zigzag stitching are done the netting will be attached to the base fabric.

4. Cut away the base fabric from the openings on the right side of the fabric and the excess netting from the wrong side (**fig. 40**).

5. Finish with the final satin stitching to encase the raw edges (**fig. 41**).

Free Motion Embroidery for Support

Straight stitch free motion embroidery can be used to fill a cut away area eliminating the need for bars to connect the edges. This is especially helpful for large cut away areas. Stitches will be placed in the open space and on top of the WSS.

1. Have at least two layers of WSS behind the base fabric.

2. Do the straight stitching and the narrow open zigzag as described above.

3. Cut away the base fabric from the opening being careful to leave the WSS (**fig. 42**).

4. Set up the machine for machine embroidery. Place the open darning foot or darning spring on the machine. Lower the feed dogs. Thread tension should be balanced or the top thread tension slightly loosened.

5. The fabric is in a hoop.

6. Pull up bobbin thread and tie-on at the edge of the open area (**fig. 43**).

7. Straight stitch on top of the WSS in the open space by running the machine at a steady moderate speed. These stitches should overlap each other AND pierce the edge of the base fabric often so that when the WSS is washed away, the stitches will hold together (**fig. 44**). This stitching can be rather dense or more open and airy.

8. After this stitching is done, replace the darning foot with the appliqué foot and raise the feed dogs. Reset the machine for a satin stitch.

9. Satin stitch the edges of the opening (**fig. 45**). ▨

Normandy Lace is a term referring to lace shaping on netting fabric. I have seen antique doilies, pillows, tablecloths and blouses made using this method.

Normandy Lace

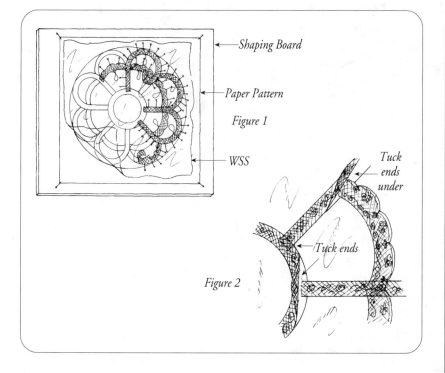

Shaping Board

Paper Pattern

Figure 1

WSS

Tuck ends under

Tuck ends

Figure 2

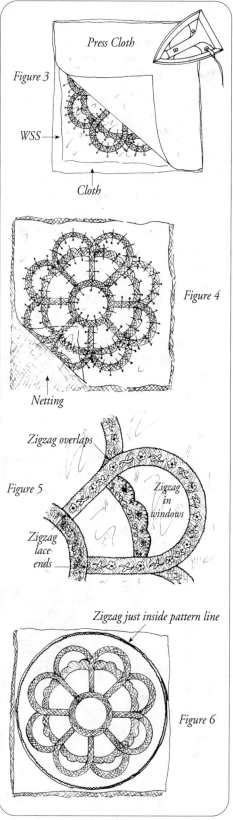

Press Cloth

Figure 3

WSS

Cloth

Figure 4

Netting

Zigzag overlaps

Figure 5

Zigzag in windows

Zigzag lace ends

Zigzag just inside pattern line

Figure 6

I. Lace Shaping

1. Trace the template on paper, using a permanent marking pen.

2. Place the template paper on a lace shaping board.

3. Place a piece of Solvy (Water Soluble Stabilizer-WSS) over the template. Pin.

4. Shape the lace over the WSS using the techniques for lace shaping (**fig. 1**). The laces should be placed on the WSS from bottom to top. In other words, all the lace pieces that fall under other lace pieces should be shaped in place first. Make sure all the ends of the lace pieces are tucked under another piece of lace (**fig. 2**).

5. After shaping, re-pin (pinning flat) the shaped lace to the WSS.

6. Place a press cloth on the top and bottom of the WSS/lace shaping. Press the lace into the WSS with just enough steam (very light steam) to stick the lace to the WSS (**fig. 3**).

II. Embroidery - Method I

1. Cut one piece of netting larger than the pattern piece.

2. Place the lace work on top of the netting. Place a press cloth on the top and bottom of the pieces. Press with just enough steam to stick the layers together (**fig. 4**).

3. Zigzag along the edges of each lace "window." When the lace intersects, zigzag across the intersection following the piece of lace on top (**fig. 5**).

4. Make sure all lace ends are zigzagged in place (see **fig. 5**).

5. Trace pattern lines on netting/WSS, using a tiny zigzag, stitch just inside the pillow or garment pattern lines (**fig. 6**).

6. Work embroidery stitches in the "windows," if desired. Note: if more stabilizer is required for machine decorative stitches press extra layers of WSS to the back of the netting (**fig.** 7).

7. Trim along the pattern lines. Do not cut the stitching. Soak in water to remove the WSS.

8. If the embroidery placed in a "window" is crooked or not to your liking, simply cut the netting from the "window" close to the zigzag stitches. Embroider a stabilized piece of netting larger than the "window." Place the new embroidered netting piece in the opening and stitch in place with a zigzag (**fig.** 8). Cut the excess netting outside the edges of the "window".

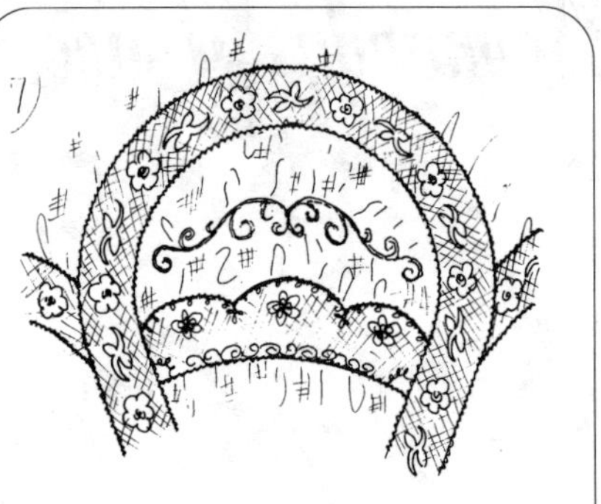

Figure 7

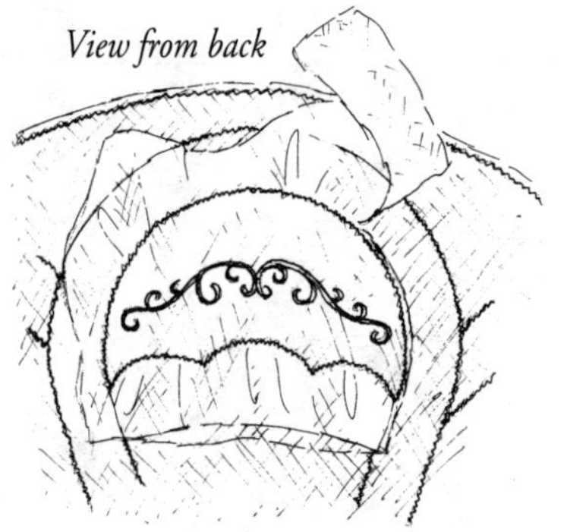

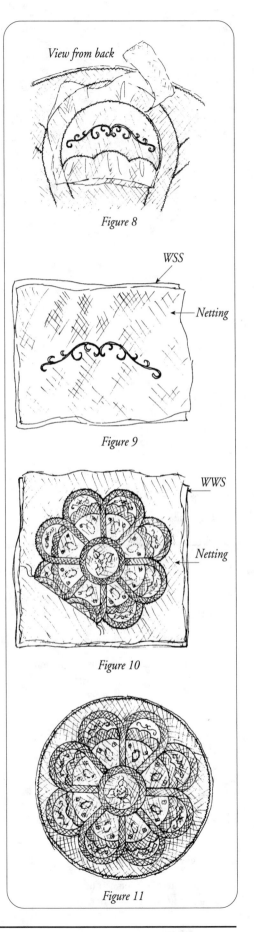

Figure 8

Method II

1. Cut pieces of netting larger than the "window" created by the shaped lace. Press pieces of netting to some WSS as described above. Work embroidery stitches on the netting/WSS (**fig.** 9). Note: if no embroidery is desired in a window, simply follow directions omitting the embroidery.

2. Center the embroidered netting under the "windows" and stitch in place along the edge of the lace using a small zigzag (**see fig.** 8). Trim the excess netting/WSS from behind the lace. Complete the entire design using this method.

3. Zigzag over any areas where the lace crossed, but was not stitched in place with the netting (**see fig.** 5).

4. Remove the excess WSS around the edges of the design. Soak in water to remove the WSS.

5. If additional netting is required along the outer edges of the design to fit the pillow or garment pattern cut a piece of netting larger than the pattern piece. Place the Normandy lace piece in the desired position and zigzag along the outer edge of the design. The excess netting can be trimmed from underneath the lace design (**fig. 10**).

6. Cut pattern from Normandy lace and netting fabric (**fig.** 11). ✻

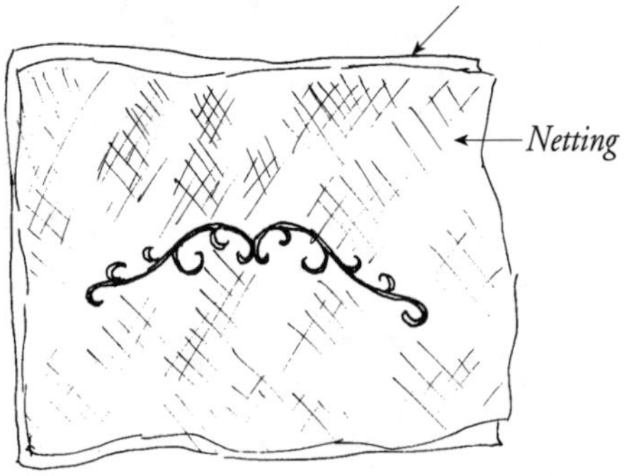

Figure 9

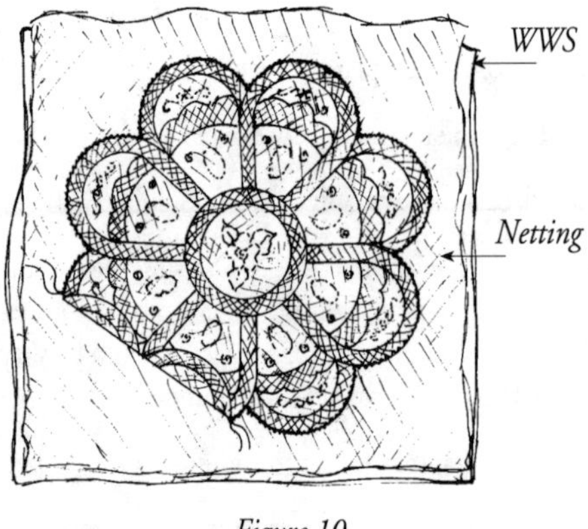

Figure 10

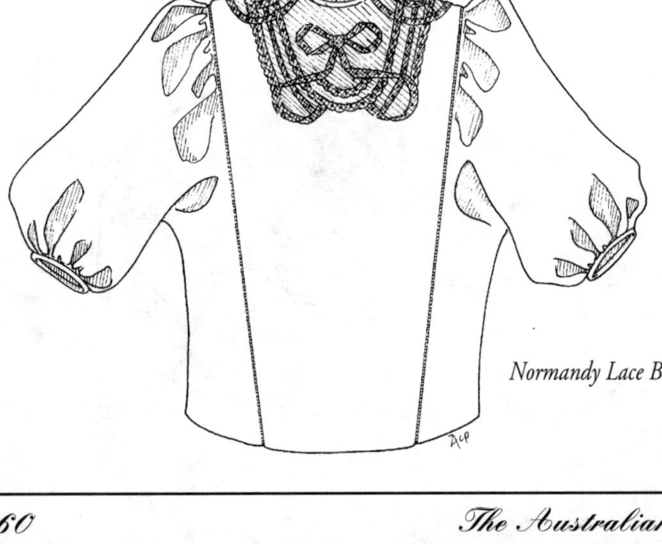

Normandy Lace Blouse

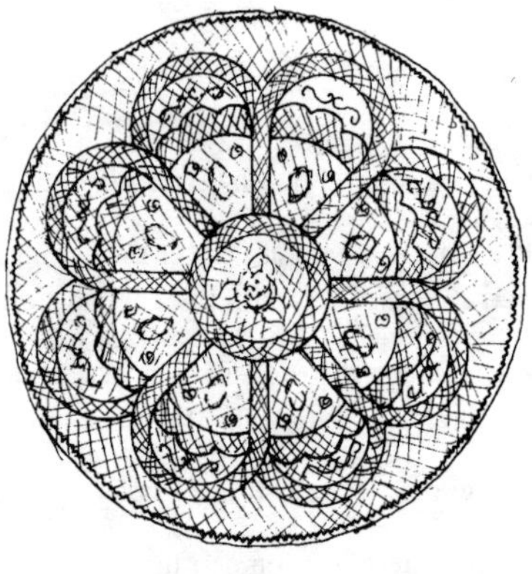

Figure 11

Seminole Patchwork

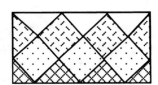

Seminole Patchwork

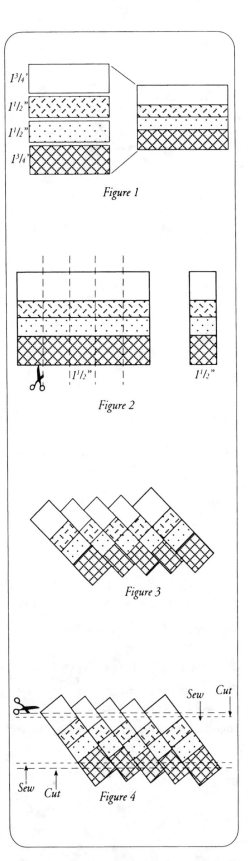

Materials Required

❋ Fabric strips of different colors and/or lace insertion pieces.

❋ Note: In the example given below the $1^1/_2$" by 45" strips will make about 18" of Seminole patchwork.

Directions

1. Making the Seminole patchwork strips - All strips are usually the width of the fabric by the following measurements: Inside strips will need to be cut $^1/_2$" wider than the desired finished width. The two outside will need to be $^1/_4$" wider than the inside strips. For example, if the finished inner strips are to be $^3/_4$", cut the inner strips to $1^1/_2$". Therefore the outer strips will be cut to $1^3/_4$". Note: cutting needs to be very precise.

2. Stitch the inside pieces together to form one multi-colored strip 45" long (all seams $^1/_4$"). Stitch the wider strips to the outer edges of the multi-colored strip. **Note:** stitching needs to be very precise (**fig. 1**).

3. Cut the multi-colored strip into pieces the same width as the original inner strips. Using the example, cut pieces to $1^1/_2$" (**fig 2**).

4. Place two multi-colored pieces, right sides together, lining up the seams, off setting each piece by one square. Pin in place. Stitch together using a $^1/_4$" seam.

5. Repeat for the remaining pieces. When the strip is turned vertically (squares look like diamonds) each color lines up, top to bottom (point to point) (**fig. 3**). The un-stitched pieces on each side of the patchwork piece will be trimmed off when the piece is complete.

6. Trim off each side of the patchwork strip $^1/_4$" from the points of the last inside piece (**fig. 4**).

7. Stitch into the project using a $^1/_4$" seam.

Note: Lace can be added to the pieced strip, if desired. The pieces can be stitch together without the seams matching for an different appearance. ❋

Ribbon and Organdy Sandwiches

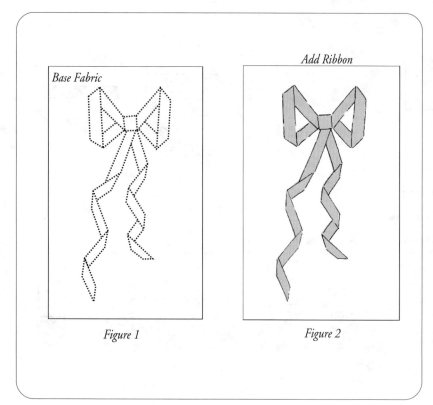

Base Fabric

Add Ribbon

Figure 1

Figure 2

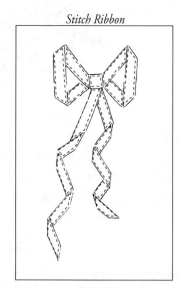

Stitch Ribbon

Figure 3

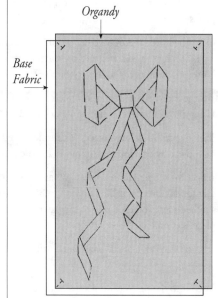

Organdy

Base
Fabric

Figure 4

Materials Required

❋ Base Fabric

❋ Organdy

❋ Ribbon

Directions

1. Trace the template for the design on the base fabric (**fig.1**).

2. Shape the ribbon along the template lines (**fig. 2**). Using the flip flop method found on page 44.

3. Stitch the ribbon in place using a straight stitch or small zigzag (**fig 3**).

4. Place the organdy over the ribbon/fabric. Pin the organdy to the base fabric and treat as one layer of fabric (**fig. 4**).

Note: Lace can be used in place of ribbon, if desired. ❋

Spoke Collar

Directions

1. Trace the collar pattern on a piece of fabric larger than the collar (fig. 1).

2. Place strips of lace along the template lines that radiate from the neck, allowing the lace to extend into the neckline and into the drawn scalloped lines. Do not place a strip along the center backs of the collar. Pin in place. Zigzag each strip to the collar along the outer edges of the lace (fig. 2).

3. Starting at the center back of the collar, shape lace along the template lines for the insertion lace, continue around the scallops. Refer to the Mitering Lace and Lace Scallops.

4. Stitch the <u>inside edge</u> of the lace to the collar using a small, tight zigzag. Do not stitch along the outer edge of the lace (fig. 3).

5. Trim the fabric from behind the lace and zigzag each miter fold of the scalloped lace (fig. 4).

6. Attach entredeux along the outer edge of the insertion lace scallops (fig. 5).

7. Gather edging lace to fit the outer edge of the collar. Butt the gathered lace to the entredeux. Zigzag (fig. 6).

8. Press the finished collar.

9. Place the collar on the blouse with the neck edge of the collar to the neck of the blouse. Pin in place and finish the neck using the General Blouse Directions, II. Neck Finishes, A Bias Binding.

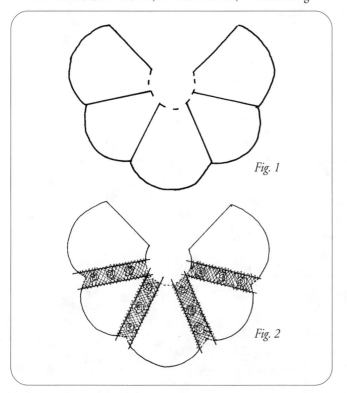

Fig. 1

Fig. 2

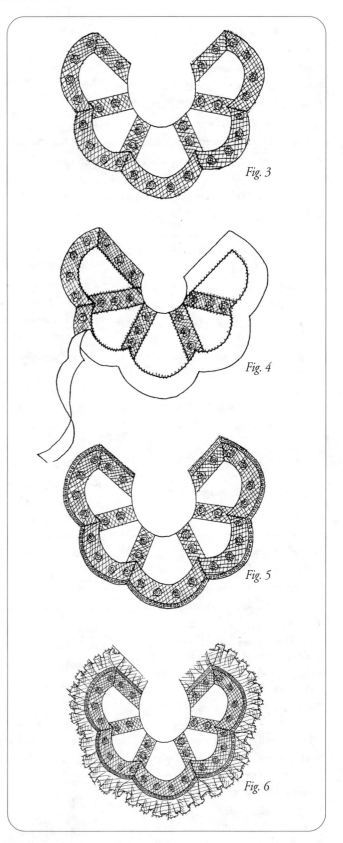

Fig. 3

Fig. 4

Fig. 5

Fig. 6

Index